# The Old Wives' Tale

CW00839932

*Oxford Progressive English Readers* provide a wide range of enjoyable reading at six language levels. Text lengths range from 8,000 words at the Starter level, to about 35,000 words at Level 5. The latest methods of text analysis, using specially designed software, ensure that readability is carefully controlled.

The aim of the series is to present stories to engage the interest of the reader; to intrigue, mystify, amuse, delight and stimulate the imagination.

# The Old Wives' Tale

**Arnold Bennett**

OXFORD
UNIVERSITY PRESS

# OXFORD
### UNIVERSITY PRESS

Oxford University Press is a department of the University of Oxford.
It furthers the University's objective of excellence in research, scholarship,
and education by publishing worldwide in

Oxford  New York

Auckland  Cape Town  Dar es Salaam  Hong Kong  Karachi
Kuala Lumpur  Madrid  Melbourne  Mexico City  Nairobi
New Delhi  Shanghai  Taipei  Toronto

With offices in

Argentina  Austria  Brazil  Chile  Czech Republic  France  Greece
Guatemala  Hungary  Italy  Japan  South Korea  Poland  Portugal
Singapore  Switzerland  Thailand  Turkey  Ukraine  Vietnam

Oxford is a registered trade mark of Oxford University Press

© Oxford University Press 2008

First published 1995
Second edition published 2008

This impression (lowest digit)
1  3  5  7  9  11  13  15  14  12  10  8  6  4  2

Retold by L A Hill

Illustrated by K Y Chan

Syllabus design and text analysis by David Foulds

ISBN  978-0-19-546259-3

Printed in Hong Kong
Published by Oxford University Press (China) Ltd
18th Floor, Warwick House East, Taikoo Place, 979 King's Road, Quarry Bay
Hong Kong

# Contents

# Introduction

*T*he *Old Wives' Tale* is neither funny nor sad; it is not an adventure story or a mystery novel. It is all these things put together in a compelling story of two sisters, Constance and Sophia Baines. Constance is meek and mild-mannered; Sophia is rebellious and romantic.

Set in the small provincial town of Bursley in mid-Victorian England, *The Old Wives' Tale* follows the sisters' lives from youth to old age. The setting ranges from their mother's draper's shop to the shady areas of Paris, the action ranges from the domestic routine of the Baines household to the siege of Paris during the Franco-Prussian War. As the sisters continue their separate lives, they both learn how to find happiness and deal with life's disappointments.

Arnold Bennett spent his childhood in English towns before living in Paris for eight years. *The Old Wives' Tale* was published during his French days. It draws on his experience of life in these places and is generally regarded as Bennett's finest work.

## About Arnold Bennett

Arnold Bennett (1867–1931) was born in Hanley, a provincial town in the central part of England. The family moved house several times and the boy went to several schools in the area.

After winning a writing competition, Bennett was encouraged to take up work in the media. He became assistant editor of a magazine in 1894. His first novel, *A Man from the North*, appeared four years later, and its success allowed him to become a full-time writer. He went to live in Paris in 1903, spending the next eight years there writing novels and plays. In 1908, *The Old Wives' Tale* was published and was well received.

It is believed that Bennett wanted to bring the French 'realistic' manner of writing into the English novel. He remarked that *The Old Wives' Tale* was inspired by *Une Vie*, the first novel of the French writer Maupassant. Many of Bennett's stories are set in the scenery of his childhood, about the lives of ordinary people.

Bennett died in 1931 from illness and his ashes were buried in his home town.

# 1
# The Two Sisters

## The draper's daughters

Constance and Sophia Baines were sisters. They lived with their mother and father in an industrial town called Bursley, in England. At the time when this story begins, in 1862, Constance was sixteen and Sophia was fifteen. 5

Constance was not as beautiful as her younger sister, but both girls were charming and full of life. They combined innocence with intelligence, good manners with occasional storms of emotion, and a complete lack of knowledge about some things with surprising wisdom in others. 10

The girls' father John Baines was a draper; his business was making and selling clothes. Baines's draper's shop, at Number 4 St Luke's Square, had been famous in Bursley for a long time. John Baines himself was an invalid. He had had a stroke which had left him half paralysed, and his condition 15 was incurable. Ever since then, he had been unable to move around easily, and for the past twelve years he had spent most of his time in bed. Despite this, John Baines was one of the most respected people in Bursley.

The Baineses had a big, ugly servant called Maggie. She 20 was continually falling in love, getting engaged and then deciding not to marry.

One Thursday afternoon, which was Maggie's afternoon off, Constance and Sophia were looking out of the window of the shop, and watching her. She was talking to a man in the 25 square—her latest boyfriend.

'It's too silly!' said Sophia severely. Then, as she had nothing to do after Maggie and her boyfriend had walked away, she picked up a dress that Mrs Baines had been making for herself and went behind a big mirror. 30

'What are you doing there, Sophia?' Constance asked.

'I'm not doing anything.'

'You're not putting Mother's dress on?'

'Why not?'

'Mother will punish you, I can tell you!'

Sophia jumped out from behind the mirror with a naughty look on her face. She admired herself in the glass. She looked very mature. She was proud of her appearance. Then she stepped back, and not being used to the long dress, she tripped on the lower part of the skirt and fell over.

Constance ran to her sister and helped her to get up. 'Oh, Sophia,' she said, laughing but worried at the same time, 'I do hope you haven't done anything to that dress—'

Suddenly, the two girls heard groans coming from behind the door at the back of the shop. They looked at each other in surprise. Then the door opened. A young man came in, holding his face with both hands. When he saw the girls in the shop, he quickly put his hands behind his back, stopped groaning and pretended that he was quite all right. 'Oh, I beg your pardon!' he said, and left the room quickly.

## Mr Povey's tooth

The young man was Samuel Povey. He did the work in the shop that Mr Baines was unable to do because of his illness. He was the shop manager. Mr Povey was a quiet man. He was not tall, or good-looking, or interesting to talk to, but he was faithful and efficient in his work.

The girls began to laugh nervously. 'I thought he'd gone to the dentist,' Constance whispered.

Mr Povey had had toothache for two days. He had told everyone that he was going to the dentist that Thursday afternoon. Mr Povey was always saying that people who delayed going to the dentist were only storing up trouble for themselves, but in fact this time he was really afraid to go.

While Sophia changed back into her own dress, Constance checked that their mother's dress had not been damaged.

'Shouldn't we do something for Mr Povey?' Constance suggested.

'Let's see if he's in his room,' said Sophia.

The two girls went and knocked at the door of Mr Povey's room, but there was no reply. They went in. The room was empty. They were just leaving when he reappeared.

'Oh, Mr Povey!' said Constance. 'We were looking for you.' 5

'To see if we could do anything for you,' Sophia added.

'Oh, no, thanks!' said Mr Povey.

'You haven't been to the dentist,' said Constance sympathetically. 10

'No,' said Mr Povey. 'I thought it was going to rain, and if I'd got wet—you see—and cold ...'

'You should keep warm,' Constance agreed. 'Why don't you go into the sitting room? There's a fire there.'

'Well, all right, I will, thank you,' said Mr Povey. 15

The girls followed him in, and they all sat down. Mr Povey was clearly suffering.

'I suppose you haven't got anything for this toothache, have you?' he asked. 'Laudanum will do. If I just sipped a little, without swallowing it, I think it would ease the pain.' 20

'There's sure to be some in Mother's cupboard,' said Sophia, and the girls went to get it. When they found it, they were worried to see the word POISON on the label.

'Just two or three drops in a little water,' said Mr Povey when they brought it to him.

Sophia fetched the water. Constance carefully poured out the laudanum, but by mistake she put four drops in instead of three. Mr Povey took it, sipped some eagerly and lay down on the sofa.

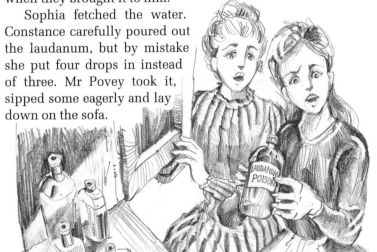

The girls watched him, afraid that they might have poisoned him. After a while, Constance said, 'Surely he hasn't swallowed it!'

'He's asleep now, anyhow,' said Sophia.

Mr Povey certainly was asleep. The question in Constance's mind was: would he ever wake up again?

Mr Povey's mouth was wide open, so Sophia looked in. 'Oh, Con,' she said to her sister, 'do come and look!'

In one corner of Mr Povey's mouth was a large broken tooth. It was loose.

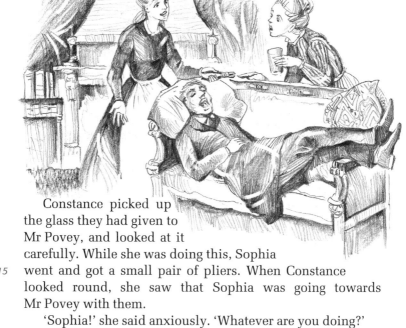

Constance picked up the glass they had given to Mr Povey, and looked at it carefully. While she was doing this, Sophia went and got a small pair of pliers. When Constance looked round, she saw that Sophia was going towards Mr Povey with them.

'Sophia!' she said anxiously. 'Whatever are you doing?'

'Nothing,' answered Sophia.

A moment later, Mr Povey woke with a jump. He sat up and looked at the girls rather thoughtfully. 'My tooth's much better,' he said.

Sophia was trembling from head to foot with hidden laughter.

'What are you laughing at?' Constance demanded.

Sophia secretly showed her the pliers. Between their points was Mr Povey's broken tooth.

'What!' Constance cried, finding it difficult to believe what her sister had done, but Sophia gave her a hard push to remind her that Mr Povey could hear.

It was time to take tea up to their father's room. There was always someone in the room to look after him; he was never left alone. On Thursday afternoons, it was the turn of his oldest and closest friend, Mr Critchlow. Mr Critchlow owned the chemists' shop next door. He would often give everyone his advice on health and medicine, and he took a particular interest in looking after Mr Baines.

The girls took some tea to their father and Mr Critchlow. Then they went down to have theirs with Mr Povey. They all had something to eat, too.

While he was eating, Mr Povey suddenly cried, 'My God! I've swallowed it!'

'Swallowed what, Mr Povey?' Constance asked. Sophia's face had turned bright red.

'That broken tooth! It has been loose for two years,' said Mr Povey. 'I've just swallowed it with my food.'

'Oh, Mr Povey!' Constance cried. And then she added, 'At least it can't hurt you any more now.'

'But it wasn't that tooth that was hurting me,' said Mr Povey. 'It's another one, on the other side.'

Sophia could not stay there any longer. She wanted to laugh so much that she almost burst. She put her cup down on the table so quickly that she spilt the tea. Then she ran straight out of the room.

### The quarrel

When Constance went to the bedroom she shared with Sophia later that night, Sophia was already in bed. 'Well,' Sophia said teasingly, 'how's darling Mr Povey?'

'Asleep,' said Constance. 'At least Mother thinks so. When she got home, she went to see how he was, but when she knocked at his door, there was no answer.'

On hearing that, Sophia exploded into laughter. She laughed on and on while Constance stared at her.

'I don't know what's come over you!' said Constance.

'It's only because I can't even think about this without going into fits!' Then Sophia held up a tiny object in her left hand.

Constance frowned, and her face became bright red. 'You don't mean to say you've kept it! How nasty you are, Sophia! Give it to me at once and let me throw it away!'

'No,' said Sophia, still laughing. 'I wouldn't part with it for anything. It's too lovely.'

'Sophia, I'm ashamed of you. Give it to me.' Constance held out her hand for Sophia to put the tooth on it.

Till then Sophia had not noticed how serious her sister was. She was surprised and also a little afraid, but this only lasted for a second. Sophia was by nature much braver than Constance.

Suddenly a battle began. The beauty of Sophia and the serious tenderness of Constance changed into something threatening and cruel. Sophia got up, put the piece of tooth in her workbox, and then went back to bed, looking at her sister as if daring her to do anything.

Five minutes later, when she had finished combing her hair and was ready for bed, Constance went straight to Sophia's workbox, got the tooth and threw it out of the window.

'There!' she said defiantly.

Sophia was completely shocked. The girls regarded their workboxes as private. Neither would dare open and search through the box of the other without permission, let alone take something from it. Constance had broken the code of honour between them.

In Sophia's eyes, her elder sister was the kindest, sweetest, most honourable person she knew. Yet in a single moment, Constance had smashed one of her chief standards of behaviour. It was outrageous.

Seeing the look on Sophia's face, Constance realized what she had done. It frightened them both.

## Leaving school

Mrs Baines was a fat, attractive woman with calm, confident eyes. One Friday morning, she was in the kitchen making pastry with Sophia when she said to her, 'Has Constance talked to you about leaving school?'

'Yes,' Sophia answered curtly.

'Well, what do you think? Are you glad? You're quite old enough to leave, you know. And as we've decided already that Constance should leave, it would be much simpler if you both left at the same time.'

'Mother, what am I going to do after I've left school?'

'I hope that both of you will do whatever you can to help me—and your father, of course.'

'I don't want to work in the shop, Mother,' Sophia said nervously.

'Then what will you do? Your father and I were hoping you would want to repay us for all the—'

Sophia refused to accept that a parent had done a child the greatest favour by bringing it into the world. 'I don't really want to leave school,' she said.

'But you will have to sooner or later,' argued Mrs Baines.

'Yes, I know,' answered Sophia. 'And then I should like to be a teacher.'

'Your father wouldn't like that. It wouldn't be suitable.'

'Why not, Mother?'

Mrs Baines was surprised. It was not because Sophia was being difficult; Mrs Baines was used to that. What surprised her was that Sophia wanted to go into teaching. 'You would have to live away from home too much,' she explained.

'Oh, that wouldn't be a problem,' Sophia replied. 'Miss Chetwynd would let me work with her for a while, here in Bursley. Then I could stay with her sister who has a big school in London.' Miss Chetwynd was Sophia's teacher.

'Oh dear, Sophia! Instead of getting better as you grow older, you know, you're getting worse,' Mrs Baines remarked. 'I do wish you could be more like your sister.' Sophia continued helping her mother in silence. As soon as the pastry was finished, she went to her room and stayed there all afternoon.

Mrs Baines finally shamed the unwilling Mr Povey into going to the dentist and having his tooth out. At supper that evening, he could only eat soft food. Sophia had no appetite; she only pretended to eat. Each time she tried to swallow, the tears came to her eyes. Her talk with her mother that morning had badly upset her. She really did not want to leave school and start working in the shop.

Early the next morning, Sophia was still sulking. She was standing at the window in the girls' bedroom looking out on the square when her mother came in. 'Sophia, you'll die of cold if you stand there like that. Get back into bed, dear.'

When Sophia obeyed, Mrs Baines brought her a small cup and spoon.

'What's that, Mother?' Sophia asked.

'Just a little medicine, my dear,' Mrs Baines answered.

'I don't want it, Mother,' said Sophia. 'I'm quite well.'

They argued for some time. It was just a small thing to argue about, but it was also a battle of wills. Finally, Mrs Baines said, 'Well, I can't force you to take it. You're a big girl now, but you are also a naughty girl. If you want to be ill, then I suppose you must.' She left the room.

In the middle of the morning, Mrs Baines and Constance were looking out of the window when they saw Sophia walking alone across the square. They could hardly believe their eyes. The Baines girls scarcely ever went out without permission, and never alone.

After dinner, Mrs Baines said to Sophia, 'What were you doing out in the town this morning?'

Sophia refused to answer.

'Do you want me to have to smack you, child?' Mrs Baines was beginning to get angry.

Sophia began to sob. 'I just went out,' she said at last.

'Why did you go out? Now tell me quickly! I can't wait all day for an answer.'

'I don't know,' Sophia murmured, and began to sob even louder.

'Sophia, I'm not going to let you talk to me like this. If you think because you're leaving school, you can do exactly as you like—'

'But I don't want to leave school!' shouted Sophia resentfully. 'Oh, you all just want to make me miserable!' She 5 ran out, and went upstairs to her room.

## Miss Chetwynd

On Sunday afternoon, Sophia was in bed with a feverish cold. Mrs Baines was in the girls' bedroom, looking after her. She happened to look out of the window. What she saw made 10 her go downstairs and start taking her best tea things out the cupboard. 'Maggie!' she called out.

When Maggie answered, Mrs Baines told her to take the tea things and put them on the sitting room table. Just then there was a knock at the street door. Maggie went to see who 15 it was, and Mrs Baines went and waited in the sitting room. Maggie returned with a visitor.

'Ah, Miss Chetwynd,' Mrs Baines said, 'I'm delighted to see you. I noticed you crossing the square, and I hoped you might call on us.' 20

Miss Chetwynd was about forty, thin and rather poor. Mrs Baines pitied her because she herself was a married woman with two lovely daughters, and she was never short of money. On the other hand, Miss Chetwynd came from a higher class of family—one which looked down upon 25 shopkeepers like the Baineses. It was impossible to decide which of the two women felt more important than the other.

They began to talk. Soon Miss Chetwynd asked Mrs Baines whether she had heard that her sister Elizabeth was engaged to marry the Reverend Archibald Jones. 30

Mrs Baines said she had not, and was most surprised. Archibald Jones was well known in most parts of England as a popular preacher. He lived in London but went all over the country talking to the people about religion. He was about fifty. Now Elizabeth Chetwynd, who had left Bursley 35 twenty-five years before at the age of twenty, had caught him! She was a rather severe woman, and far from good-looking, but she was very clever. Obviously, thought Mrs Baines, Archibald Jones admired her mind.

The two women talked about Constance and Sophia.

5 'It is quite true that Sophia is as clever as Constance,' said Miss Chetwynd, 'and she has the most striking character I have ever come across. My sister likes her very much too, you know. She has mentioned her to Mr Jones.'

'I suppose your sister will give up her school in London
10 now,' said Mrs Baines.

'Oh, no!' Miss Chetwynd was quite shocked. 'Archibald takes the greatest interest in the school!'

'Then do you think Sophia would make a good teacher?' asked Mrs Baines. Although this had nothing to do directly
15 with what they had just been discussing, the words marked a turning point in Mrs Baines's mind. In a small way, she had surrendered. She knew she would have to let Sophia go if she wanted to.

'Sophia would make an excellent teacher,' said
20 Miss Chetwynd.

Constance had slipped into the room, unable to resist the temptation of finding out what was going on. She was supposed to be sitting with her father. She said, 'I've left both doors open, Mother. I can hear if he needs anything.'

25 Her mother rewarded her by inviting her to take part in the conversation. Soon it was agreed that Sophia should go and work for Miss Chetwynd as an assistant teacher, and perhaps she might go to London later on. Mrs Baines secretly feared that such a thing might happen, but with the Reverend
30 Archibald Jones there, it did not seem quite so bad.

Some nights later, when the girls were talking before falling asleep, Sophia said to Constance, 'I went to Miss Chetwynd and asked her to come and talk to Mother.'

Constance was surprised. Fancy her sister going out alone
35 on that Saturday morning to get Miss Chetwynd to help her. Constance could never imagine herself doing such a thing!

# 2
# The Traveller

## The elephant

'Sophia, will you come and see the elephant? Do come!' Constance said eagerly.

'No,' said Sophia, uninterested. 'I'm much too busy.'

Two years had passed, and both girls had grown up. They 5
were now very different from each other.

Constance worked in the shop and was a great success there; she was popular both with the customers, and with the shop assistants.

Sophia was working at the school with Miss Chetwynd, 10
and was studying to be a teacher. She was not so interested in people as Constance. Miss Chetwynd was her only friend.

At home, Sophia hardly spoke much to anyone; she was often short-tempered, and could sometimes be quite unpleasant. Although she expected others to be careful about 15
how they treated her, she never bothered to treat them with the same amount of respect. But Sophia was splendidly beautiful; even her mother felt that with such good looks Sophia might partly be excused for her rudeness.

'Well,' said Constance, 'if you won't come, I shall ask 20
Mother if she will.'

Sophia did not answer. Constance left the room. In a moment, Mrs Baines walked in.

'Sophia, please go and sit with your father for a little while,' Mrs Baines said. 'Constance and I are going up to the 25
playground for a few minutes to see the elephant. You can study just as well in there as here. Your father's asleep.'

'Oh, very well,' Sophia replied. 'It will be quieter in Father's room, anyway. The noise here is terrible.'

It was the third day of the Bursley Wakes, a kind of annual 30
festival in which people enjoyed themselves in the noisiest ways. The whole centre of the town was given over to

various popular forms of amusement. Most of the square was occupied by a huge tent, where wild animals roared and growled day and night. And spread out along the road from St Luke's Square right up to the marketplace were hundreds of smaller tents where one could see displays of such things as 'The Horrors of the French Revolution'. Along the streets all around were stalls selling different kinds of food. Every pub was full of noisy, drunken people.

It was a cheerful, colourful sight, but not one that greatly pleased the leading families of Bursley. Miss Chetwynd's school was closed during the Wakes, so that the daughters of the leading families might remain safely at home until it was all over. The Baineses usually avoided the festival in every possible way, so the success of the elephant as a popular attraction would be difficult to overestimate.

The night before, one of the elephants in the large tent had suddenly knelt down on a man; it had then smashed its way out of the tent, picked up another man and tried to put him in its mouth. When its keeper tried to stop it, the elephant placed the man on the ground and stuck its tusk into his arm. It then allowed itself to be led away through the large crowd that had gathered to see what was happening.

The elephant was taken to the back of the tent and tied up with strong ropes. Someone painted a white mark on its head. Six soldiers shot it from a distance of five yards. It died at once. The crowd cheered, and the soldiers were taken away to different pubs where they were treated like heroes. 5
The body of the elephant was put on a cart and disappeared into the night. Nothing like it had ever occurred in Bursley before.

The next day, it became known that the dead elephant lay near the playground, waiting for the authorities to decide what to do with it. Everybody, rich and poor, upper class and lower class, wanted to see the huge dead animal, with its long white tusks.

'We're going now,' said Mrs Baines.

'All right,' answered Sophia, pretending to be busy with her studies. Then she heard a conversation in the passage, which greatly surprised her. 25

'Are you going up to see the elephant, Mrs Baines?'

'Yes, Mr Povey. Why?'

'I think I had better come with you. The crowd is sure to be rough.' Mr Povey spoke firmly, as if he had made a decision and would not allow Mrs Baines to change his mind. 30

'But the shop?' asked Mrs Baines.

'We shall not be long,' said Mr Povey.

'Oh yes, Mother,' Constance begged.

Sophia could not believe her ears. 'Even Mr Povey wants to go!' she thought. 35

She looked out of the window of her father's bedroom, and watched the three cross the square. This must surely be the greatest show of respect for a dead elephant, she thought.

Her mother, her sister and even the shop manager of Baines's were all going to honour it! It was simply astonishing. Sophia realized that she had made a mistake about the importance of that elephant.

<sub>5</sub>                              **The face of an angel**

While Sophia was at the window, she noticed a young man coming up King Street. He was followed by a porter carrying some luggage. She blushed. Clearly this young man had stirred up feelings in her that were rather special.

<sub>10</sub>    She looked quickly at her father. He was asleep. He was a complete invalid now, and had to be fed and looked after like a baby. He slept for hours even in the day time. Sophia left the room. She ran down into the shop. The three young lady assistants there were highly astonished to see her; for

<sub>15</sub>    Miss Sophia to come into the shop was most unusual.

In the corner of the shop near the window, there was a place that had been divided off from the rest with a row of large flower boxes. It was known as 'Miss Baines's corner'. Sophia went and sat there and pretended to be looking for

<sub>20</sub>    something. When she heard a voice near the door of the shop asking first for Mr Povey and then for Mrs Baines, she stood up. She caught hold of the object nearest to her, which happened to be a pair of scissors. She hurried towards the showroom stairs, pretending she had found what she wanted,

<sub>25</sub>    and was on her way back to her father's room. She wanted to stop and turn round, but something prevented her. She was at the foot of the stairs when one of the assistants said, 'I suppose you don't know when Mr Povey and your mother are likely to be back, Miss Sophia? Here's—'

<sub>30</sub>    Sophia turned round suddenly. 'They're—I—' she stammered. She was holding on to the stair rail. The young man she had seen in the street came boldly forwards.

'Good morning, Miss Sophia,' he said. 'It is a long time since I had the pleasure of seeing you.'

<sub>35</sub>    Never had she blushed as she blushed then. She hardly knew what she was doing.

The young man was Gerald Scales. He worked as a travelling sales representative for Birkinshaws—the largest and most famous of all the Manchester cloth companies. He was rather short, about thirty, and had fair hair. He had been working for Birkinshaws for several years. To Sophia, he 5 looked mature and important.

Sophia had only seen him once before when she was quite a little girl, but she had never forgotten him. She had thought of him as the perfect young man, well dressed, well mannered, and elegant. 10

Seeing him again had an amazing effect on her. She was not the same Sophia as she had been minutes before. Her beautiful face, usually ill-tempered and unkind, had now changed into the face of an angel. No one who looked at her could have believed that she was not always so sweet and 15 perfect. Could that gentle voice ever be hard? Could those warm, loving eyes ever be cold and full of hate? Impossible! And, as Mr Scales looked at her, he surrendered.

'I see it's your Wakes here,' he said. He spoke politely, but his tone of voice showed that he did not really care for the 20 Wakes. Sophia loved him for this. She scorned everything local, and met so few people who felt the same way.

'What's this about an elephant?' Mr Scales went on.

'Well,' she said, 'of course we have never seen anything like it before in Bursley.' She smiled in gentle pity at poor 25 Bursley, and Mr Scales smiled too. They both understood that for Bursley to get so excited over a dead elephant just showed what a poor sort of place Bursley must be.

Mr Scales said. 'If I come back at about two—'

'Oh, yes, they will have returned by then,' she said. 30

'Well, goodbye.' Mr Scales smiled at her, and walked out of the shop.

Sophia felt drunk. Thoughts were rolling about in her head like things that had got loose in a storm-swept ship. 'Only just now have I really begun to live!' she thought at last. As she 35 went back to her father's room, she tried to wonder how, without letting her mother realize anything special was happening, she might see Mr Scales when he returned.

## 'You've killed your father'

When Sophia reached the bedroom, she saw that something was wrong. Her father seemed to be leaning across the far side of the bed. Frightened, she ran round. There she saw that
5 her father's head was hanging upside down close to the floor. His face, neck and hands were dark blue. His mouth was open, and his tongue was hanging out between black, swollen lips. His eyes were open and staring. The fact was that Mr Baines had woken up, and, being restless, he had slid
10 partly out of bed. Unable to use his arms or legs, he could not get back, and in that position he could not breathe. He had died of suffocation.

Sophia was filled with horror, despair and shame. She had only been out of the room for ten minutes. Why had he
15 woken up just then!

She ran out of the room and screamed, 'Maggie!'

'Yes, Miss.'

'Fetch Mr Critchlow at once. Be quick. It's Father—'

Maggie hurried away, leaving Sophia to think alone.
20 A few minutes later Mr Critchlow arrived. He took one look and immediately told Maggie to go and get the doctor. Then he turned to Sophia, 'How did this happen?'

'I was out of the room. I just ran down to the shop—'

'Oh! Playing about with that young Scales, I suppose,
25 were you? I saw him come in,' said Mr Critchlow fiercely. 'Well, you've killed your father. That's all!'

Mrs Baines's voice could be heard; she was coming up the stairs.

'And I suppose she went to see the elephant!' said
30 Mr Critchlow. He was deeply angry. His dear old friend had died because of the carelessness of those who should have been looking after him. When Mrs Baines walked into the room, he said to her, 'Well, you're a widow now, madam! She let him fall out of bed!'

35 'Mother,' cried Sophia, 'I only ran down to the shop to—to—' But Sophia could say no more. Her shame and sorrow were too much to bear.

Her husband's death did not come as a great shock to Mrs Baines. Everyone in the family had been warned of the danger of leaving him alone. Sophia, who had been asked to look after him for just a short while, had ignored the warning. Well, that was just the sort of thing Sophia would do. Mrs Baines blamed herself as much as anyone; she had expected too much of Sophia.

Sophia would not go to the funeral; she was too upset. When Mrs Baines got home afterwards, she found her younger daughter in the sitting room. The girl gave a terrible sob and threw herself into her mother's arms.

'Mother,' she cried passionately, 'Mother, I want to stop working at the school. I will do anything to please you. I'll work in the shop if you wish!'

'Keep calm, my pet,' said Mrs Baines tenderly, stroking her daughter's hair. It was a triumph for the mother at a time when she badly needed one.

## A passionate, proud girl

Two years had passed. It was the morning of the last day of the year, and a Sunday. Constance was helping Mr Povey get the shop ready for the coming week. They were making labels that would be pinned to the clothes displayed in the shop window. He watched her carefully as she wrote words like 'Cheap', 'Latest' and 'Delicate' on the pieces of coloured card.

This was a new idea for Baines's. Constance and Mr Povey were certain that the labels would improve business. Mrs Baines, however, had not been asked, and she disagreed with anything new.

When she had come down to go to chapel that morning, and found that Constance and Mr Povey were not ready because they were busy making labels, she was rude and scornful. She made them stop what they were doing.

5    Half an hour later, they were all in chapel. Mr Povey was not thinking of God, however, but about labels and the annoying ways of women. Constance, with the gentle eyes— the ideal daughter—was also not thinking of God. She was holding Mr Povey's hand, and smiling at him when she
10   thought her mother was not looking. Mrs Baines was thinking that she should make sure that she, not Mr Povey, ruled the house and the shop. Sophia's was the only mind that was concerned with more important matters.

Never was a passionate, proud girl in a more difficult
15   position! In her remorse for her deadly forgetfulness, Sophia had given up the studies that she loved and thrown herself into a way of life she hated. She knew she had not done it out of any feeling of kindness or respect towards her mother, but resentfully.

20   When Sophia had started working at the shop, there had been changes. Constance had been forced to give the millinery department over to her. Sophia's fingers had a gift that Constance's did not, for doing things with ribbons and feathers and anything else related to the decoration of ladies'
25   hats. As a milliner, Sophia was a miracle. She would be perfectly polite to customers, too, but afterwards she was usually very sharp with her mother, her sister and Mr Povey!

Sophia had spent more and more time in the shop, secretly hoping that someone special would walk in. Then
30   one day, a new sales representative for Birkinshaws had arrived, and her soul had died within her.

In chapel, Sophia admitted to herself that her reasons for going to work in the shop had been mixed. As a teacher, she might never have seen Gerald Scales again. In the shop, she
35   could not fail to meet him. But month after month had passed, and Gerald Scales had not appeared. She had felt that she had sacrificed her life for worse than nothing. She had killed her father, cheated and shamed herself with a

remorse that was not sincere—and with all that, Gerald Scales had disappeared! She was ruined.

She had become religious, and was so strict with herself about what she did that it made her whole family suffer!

Then, on this special day of the year, in the second year of 5 her shame, Mr Scales had reappeared. She had gone into the shop that morning just before they had all left for chapel, and found him talking to her mother and Mr Povey. She had shaken hands with him and run away. Nobody had noticed her blushes, and nothing had been said. Now Sophia was in 10 chapel, and Gerald Scales was in her soul!

At midnight, bells and whistles announced the arrival of the new year. As people were calling out 'Happy New Year!' to each other, the Baines family and Mr Povey crossed the square through the snow. They saw someone sitting on the 15 doorstep of Baines's.

Mr Povey ran forwards. 'It's Mr Scales!' he called back.

'Mr Scales!' cried Mrs Baines.

'Mr Scales!' murmured Sophia, terribly afraid. Perhaps she was afraid of miracles. Mr Scales sitting on their doorstep 20 certainly seemed like a miracle.

Mr Scales explained that he had been attacked on his way to the house where he was staying, but he had managed to beat the men off. He had hurt his elbow when he slipped on the snow and fell. He had had no idea that he had finished 25 up on the Baines's doorstep.

Mrs Baines said, 'You must come in, even if it's only for a minute,' and in they all went. Mr Scales was in evening dress.

Sophia was in a state of great happiness. She tried not to 30 stare at Mr Scales, but she was sure that he was the most perfect man in the world.

'I stayed in town to go to a New Year's party at Mr Lawton's,' Mr Scales explained.

Mrs Baines was impressed. Lawyer Lawton was an 35 upper-class person. He did not make friends with shopkeepers.

'My family has known Mr Lawton for a long time,' said Mr Scales.

# 3
# The Adventure

## A walk in Wedgwood Street

Sophia spent more time than usual in the shop that week. On Wednesday morning, Mr Scales appeared. He said he had come just for a moment to thank them for helping him on
5  Sunday night.

Sophia had dreamt of having a private conversation with Mr Scales as something sweetly impossible, but her mother was still upstairs, and Constance was called away to deal with a customer. Now she was alone with him. He was more
10  gentlemanly than any man she had met before.

'I suppose you don't often go out?' he said.

'I sometimes go to the Free Library,' she answered.

'On Saturdays, I suppose.'

'No, on Wednesdays,' she said and smiled. 'Usually.'
15  'It's Wednesday today. Have you been already?'

She shook her head.

At half past one, while Mrs Baines was sleeping after dinner, Sophia picked up a library book, and went out. She returned in less than twenty minutes, but her mother had
20  already woken up and was down in the shop.

Mrs Baines said, 'Have you been to the library?'

'Yes, Mother.'

'I thought you always went on Thursdays.'

'I had finished my book.'
25  The next day Mrs Baines called Sophia to her bedroom.

'Sophia,' she said sternly, 'please do not walk about the streets with young men until you have my permission.'

Sophia blushed violently. 'I—I—'

'You were seen in Wedgwood Street.'
30  'Who's been telling stories—Mr Critchlow, I suppose?' Sophia answered resentfully.

'No one has been "telling stories".'

'Well, if I meet someone by accident in the street, I can't help it, can I?' Sophia's voice shook with emotion, and she ran out of the room.

Mrs Baines remembered uneasily that it was Mr Scales who had been in the shop on the day her husband died.

## The plan

Mrs Baines's worries during the next three months were much influenced by Sophia's moods. On some days, Sophia was the old Sophia, difficult and unpleasant. On other days, she was happy, kind and content. It was on those days that Mrs Baines worried most. She did not know for sure, but she suspected that Sophia and Mr Scales were writing to each other.

In fact, Sophia's joy was caused mostly by the flaming fires that had struck her soul during a magical two minutes in Wedgwood Street. She discovered that Mr Scales had come to Bursley in the hope of meeting her. They had walked a short distance together, looking into each other's eyes. At the corner of the street, he had had to go.

'Till next time,' he had murmured. The fire of love had shot from his eyes, setting light to thoughts and feelings in Sophia's lovely head that her mother, fortunately, never even guessed about.

When the time came for Mr Scales's next visit, Mrs Baines made a plan. She decided she would be ill; that meant it would not be polite for him to come into the house. She also hinted to Constance that she should be sure to stay in the shop that morning. She warned Mr Povey not to tell anyone that Mr Scales was coming, and she arranged for Sophia to be busy seeing two customers in the showroom. At first it looked as if Mrs Baines's plan would succeed.

Usually Mr Scales was not punctual, but this time he was. Mr Povey met him and they did their business quickly. But just as Mr Povey was taking Mr Scales to the door to show him out, two lady customers came in. One went straight to Mr Povey, so Mr Povey had to leave Mr Scales. Constance came out from her corner to attend to the other. That made Mr Scales, who until then had not known Constance was in the shop, stop where he was.

5 When Constance had finished dealing with her customer, Mr Scales came across to talk to her, and they went and sat down in 'Miss Baines's corner' together. Mr Povey continued to talk to the first customer. He did not notice Sophia come down into the shop from the showroom. She joined her sister and Mr Scales in the corner.

10 When Mr Povey had finished with his customer, he noticed that Mr Scales was still inside the shop, and that he and Constance were talking happily together. He could not see Sophia from where he was standing. The conversation between Constance and Mr Scales seemed to be going on for 15 a long time, and Mr Povey became rather jealous. 'Miss Baines, your mother wants you upstairs at once,' he called out.

Constance went up to see her mother. A moment later Mr Povey, too, left the shop. On the way out, he met 20 Constance coming back. 'Where is Mother?' she asked.

Mr Povey's face was dark red. 'Oh, if you must know,' he said irritably, 'she didn't ask for you.' He then turned his back on her, and walked away.

'Then what—?' Constance began.

25 Mr Povey turned and faced her angrily. 'Haven't you been talking long enough to that—that fool?' he said. There were tears in his eyes.

Tears now fell from Constance's eyes. 'You ought to be ashamed—' she stammered.

30 Then Mrs Baines suddenly walked into the shop, and found Sophia and Mr Scales there.

## The first date

That afternoon, Sophia went out to visit Miss Chetwynd. The school finished at four, and Sophia reached the school at a 35 quarter past. She knew that Miss Chetwynd always went for a walk immediately after school, so she was not surprised

when she was told that Miss Chetwynd was out. Sophia had
not intended that Miss Chetwynd should be in.

She turned to the right and walked towards some miners'
cottages. No one else knew where she was going, or what she
planned to do. She was quite frightened at her own audacity   5
in starting on this great adventure.

That morning, just before he had left the shop, Mr Scales
had pushed a small piece of folded paper into her hand. She
had stared at it silently, blushing bright red. So, she thought,
he had written a note before he came, hoping that he would   10
be able to give it to her. He must love
her. The thought was beautiful,
but it filled her with terror!

She had put the piece of paper
in her pocket and had run upstairs,
breathless, to read it in her bedroom. The note
said that he wanted to meet her that afternoon.

On the way to her meeting, Sophia called herself wicked
and a fool, but she did not turn back. When she came to a
bridge, he was waiting for her there.   20

They were both nervous, but soon they began talking.
Sophia discovered that the reason for Mr Scales's long absence
was that he had been working for Birkinshaws in Paris. He told
her that he had been to university as a young man, that he
spoke good French; and that an uncle of his, Mr Boldero, who   25
was a partner in Birkinshaws, had got him his job there to train
him to be a partner too. Sophia was deeply impressed.

'Now tell me about yourself,' Mr Scales said.

'Oh, I'm nothing!'

'You're the finest girl I've ever met, anyhow,' declared Mr Scales.

5     She blushed and made no attempt to answer.

They walked on. Close to the side of the road, they saw a low brick wall, built in the shape of a circle. 'I expect that's an old mine shaft,' Mr Scales said. He took a stone and dropped it in. They listened. It was a long time before they
10 heard it hit the bottom. He climbed onto the wall to look down, and Sophia screamed out with fear. Mr Scales got down again. When he saw how frightened she was, he came towards her with a superior smile. 'Silly little thing!' he said.

Her fear changed suddenly to anger. She turned and began to hurry away from him. He was so surprised that at first he said nothing, and then he began to run after her.

'I didn't mean to—' he muttered, embarrassed. 'I suppose
20 I should apologize.'

'You certainly should,' she answered angrily, continuing to walk away.

'Well, I do,' he said, continuing to keep up with her.

'Please stop following me, Mr Scales,' she said, and
hurried on.

'I'll write to you,' he shouted after her.

When Sophia got home, she found her mother in the
sitting room. Mrs Baines looked up at her questioningly.     5

'You've been out, Sophia?' she asked.

'Yes, Mother. I went to see Miss Chetwynd. Where's
Constance?'

'She's not well. She's lying down.'

'Is anything the matter with her?'                          10

'No.'

This was not true. Nearly everything was the matter with
Constance at that time. But Mrs Baines had no intention of
discussing Constance's love problems with Sophia. 'And
what did Miss Chetwynd say?' she asked.                     15

'She wasn't in.'

Mrs Baines's suspicions returned at once. 'What's all that
clay on your boots, child?' she asked.

'Clay? Oh, it must be from the roads.'

'You are deceiving me, Sophia,' said Mrs Baines fiercely.   20
'Where have you been this afternoon? Have you been seeing
young Scales?'

'Yes.' The reply was both audacious and resentful.

'How did that happen?'

No answer.                                                  25

'Sophia, you heard what I said!'

Still no answer.

'Of course,' Mrs Baines went on, 'if you choose to be
wicked, neither your mother nor anyone else can stop you.
But let me warn you that Scales is a thoroughly bad young   30
man. He has been living a wild life abroad, and if his uncle
had not been a partner in Birkinshaws, he would not have
been allowed to continue working there. In the future, you
are not to go out alone. Do you understand?'

Sophia remained silent.                                     35

That night, Sophia thought about the scene at the old mine
shaft. She saw that she had been wrong to be so angry. She
remembered his words: 'You're the finest girl I ever met' and

'I shall write to you'. She fell asleep, dreaming of sweet letters from Mr Scales, and plotting how to get hold of the morning's post before Mr Povey.

## Old and beaten

In June, Aunt Harriet came over to spend a few days with Mrs Baines, who was her younger sister. Aunt Harriet lived alone, in a small village called Axe. She was very nice to Sophia, and wanted Sophia to stay with her for a while as a companion. Sophia was not at all enthusiastic, but she found herself manoeuvred into agreeing.

On the day she and Aunt Harriet left Bursley, Sophia said to her mother, 'I know why you're sending me away! But you are not being fair. You let Constance do as she pleases!'

These words disturbed Mrs Baines. Did everyone then know all about Constance and Mr Povey, she wondered. Mrs Baines really thought that she was the only one who knew, but in fact the young lady assistants in the shop hardly ever talked of anything else.

The following Sunday, after Mrs Baines, Constance and Mr Povey had had dinner together, Constance suddenly said, 'Mother, I must just run upstairs to my room.'

Mr Povey looked nervous. He waited for Constance to leave the room, and then said, 'I should like to have a word with you, Mrs Baines.'

'What about?'

'About Constance.'

'Constance?' Mrs Baines tried to sound surprised.

'I think it ought to be settled whether Constance and I are to be engaged or not.' Mr Povey spoke rather defiantly, as if he feared that Mrs Baines would be against it.

'But Mr Povey, you have never said anything to me about it until now!' Mrs Baines objected.

'All I want to know is—have you got anything against me?' he demanded. 'Do you think I'm not good enough?'

Actually that was exactly what Mrs Baines did think. Mr Povey was neither intelligent nor important. He lacked dignity. But Mrs Baines had to be careful. Mr Povey was an excellent shop manager.

'You know what a high opinion I have of you,' she said.

'I can't stay on for much longer as things are now,' Mr Povey continued. He was becoming quite emotional.

'I hope you aren't trying to threaten me,' said Mrs Baines.

'Threaten you! Do you think I would leave here without a really good reason? Of course I wouldn't. But I would leave if I couldn't stand it any longer.' Then he got up and walked quickly out of the room.

Shortly after this, a number of events occurred, compared to which the emotional problems of Mr Povey were quite unimportant.

First, a notice arrived from Birkinshaws saying that Mr Scales had been replaced by another sales representative. When she read it, Mrs Baines realized that she had sent Sophia away for nothing.

Then, suddenly Aunt Harriet arrived.

'What's the matter?' asked Mrs Baines fearfully.

'Well, what a surprise!' said Aunt Harriet. 'That's what I've driven specially over to ask you!'

'Where's Sophia?' demanded Mrs Baines.

'You don't mean to say she isn't here, Sister?' asked Aunt Harriet.

'Here? Of course she isn't here! What do you mean?'

'As soon as she got Constance's letter yesterday, saying you were ill, she came to see you.'

'I've not been ill! And Constance hasn't written to Sophia for a week or more!'

'Sister, that's impossible. Sophia has had a letter from Constance every morning. At least, she said they were from Constance. I came over myself because I thought you might be seriously ill.'

Mrs Baines's face was very pale. So was Aunt Harriet's.

'Sophia has eloped!' said Mrs Baines with icy calm. 'She has run off with that young Scales.'

Aunt Harriet called the driver of the carriage that had brought her.

'Did the driver who took Miss Sophia yesterday bring her here?' she asked.

'No, madam. He told me last night when he returned that Miss Sophia had asked him to take her to Knype Station.'

Later that afternoon, a telegram arrived. It had been sent from Charing Cross railway station, in London. It said: *I am all right, fondest love, Sophia.*

Mr Critchlow went to Manchester to find out about Scales. He returned with the news that an aunt of Scales had recently died and left him 12,000 pounds. Mr Critchlow also discovered that Scales had quarrelled with his uncle Mr Boldero and resigned from Birkinshaws.

A fortnight later, a letter came from London.

> *Dear Mother, I am married to Gerald Scales. Please don't worry about me. We are going abroad. Love to you and Constance, Sophia.*

Mrs Baines was shocked. 'My life is over,' she said. She was only just fifty, but she felt old and beaten.

Not long after this, Mrs Baines agreed to Mr Povey and Constance getting married.

Old houses see sad sights, and never forget them. One of the saddest to affect the house of John Baines at the corner of St Luke's Square and King Street, Bursley, occurred the day after Mr and Mrs Povey returned from their honeymoon. It was the sight of Mrs Baines, who had lived in that house for so long, and had had two children there and brought them up there, and who had grown there from a thin young woman to a heavy, and heavy-hearted, middle-aged lady, leaving her home with her bags and trunks and parcels to go and spend the rest of her life as the companion of her elder sister at Axe. 'Only yesterday, it seems, they were just little girls, ever so tiny, and now ...' she thought as she climbed into the carriage.

Mrs Baines went to live at Axe, the home of her childhood, content to stay there until such time as she herself would be ready for burial!

# 4
# The New Couple

## Changes

On the day that Mrs Baines left, Maggie came to see Constance. She gave her a small piece of folded paper. On it was written: *I beg to give notice that I shall leave in one month's time.* It was signed *Maggie, 10 June 1867.*

'Maggie!' Constance cried out in horror. Then she added, 'Why—?'

'I'm going to get married myself. To Mr Hollins, from the fish shop.'

When Maggie had gone, Constance ran into the shop to tell her husband the news. He was busy talking to another shopkeeper, who was a painter and decorator, so she went back to the sitting room and wrote her mother a letter. She told her that Maggie was leaving and asked what she should do. When, later that day, Samuel Povey heard the news about Maggie, he was as surprised as Constance had been.

Constance was proud of her husband Samuel (she called him 'Sam' now). She found him kind, honest and efficient in his work. However, with Mrs Baines at Axe, and Mr Povey now 'the man of the house', there were certain changes, the first of which was caused by Constance.

During their honeymoon, Samuel had worn cloth collars, but on the first day that he was back at work, she saw him take out one of the paper collars he had always worn before.

'Oh, Sam,' she cried, 'you surely aren't going to go back to wearing those horrible paper collars again!' She thought he looked ridiculous in them.

Mr Povey was sensitive to remarks about his appearance, and his face turned red with embarrassment.

'I didn't know they were "horrible",' he said sharply.

Both of them suddenly saw that they had a crisis, and stopped.

'But—' Mr Povey began.

'Just as you like, dear,' Constance said quickly. 'Please!'

'Oh, no!' he answered, trying to smile. 'It isn't really so important.' He went away with the paper collar and came
5  back with a cloth one. He never wore paper collars again.

Other changes took place. The next morning, James Boon, who was famous in that part of the country for the dogs he sold, knocked at the door. Constance answered it.

'I have heard that your husband wants a dog,' Boon said.

10  Constance had heard something about Samuel being interested in dogs, but there had never been a dog in the Baines house, and she had no idea that he wanted to buy one. However, she went to find Samuel.

Samuel came out and talked to Boon. After a while,
15  Samuel had agreed to buy a little dog just a year old. It was so loving and so timid that Constance adored it within the hour. She called it 'Fan'.

Mr Povey explained that the dog was never to go into the shop. When it did, he whipped it. Constance cried although
20  she admired her husband's firmness.

On another day, Constance discovered a box of cigars at the back of the piano. No one had ever smoked in the Baines house before, and Constance did not know that her husband did. But that day she actually saw and smelt him smoking a cigar in the room where he worked. That evening, after supper, Mr Povey openly smoked a cigar in front of his wife.

The final shock was when the signboard arrived. It was a big one—thirty-five feet long and two feet high. It was what Mr Povey had been talking about to the painter and decorator.

Old Mr Baines had always refused to have a signboard. He thought signboards were unnecessary for good shops like his. Now people wondered what Mrs Baines would say when she saw it. Constance dared not think about it, and did not mention the signboard in any of her letters. Samuel decided   5 to write and tell her himself.

## The old ways defeated

When Mrs Baines came, the visit turned out to be a pleasant one. She said nothing at all about the signboard when she arrived, and as soon as she walked into the sitting room and   10 sat down, Fan, the little dog, ran in.

Fan paused when she saw a new face, and Mrs Baines was equally surprised. The two stared at each other for a moment. Then suddenly Fan's tail began to wag, and with one jump she was up on Mrs Baines's lap. Constance gave a cry of   15 terror, 'Oh, Fan!', but Fan had settled down into that huge lap as if into heaven.

'So your name's Fan?' murmured Mrs Baines, stroking the animal. 'You're a dear!' The danger was past.

After dinner, Constance was terrified that Samuel might   20 light a cigar. She had not asked him not to, but he did not do so anyway. The only trouble came when Mrs Baines was leaving.

'You know we want you to spend Christmas with us, Mother!' Samuel said to her.   25

'I shall not!' she answered. 'Aunt Harriet and I will expect you at Axe. We've already settled that.'

There was a friendly argument, with neither side giving way. After Mrs Baines had left, Mr Povey muttered, half to himself and half to Constance, 'I shall take good care we   30 don't go there.'

Samuel Povey won the battle over Christmas through the unexpected arrival of a powerful assistant, death. Aunt Harriet died, leaving her house and her money to her sister. Mrs Baines continued for some time to refuse to   35 spend Christmas in Bursley, but in the end she gave in.

When Constance's second new servant left before Christmas, Mrs Baines offered to bring one of her own with her.

On Christmas Day, the postman brought between thirty and forty Christmas cards. One of the envelopes was addressed to *Mrs and Miss Baines* in large handwriting. Constance at once recognized it as Sophia's. The letter had come from Paris.

Mrs Baines told Constance to open it. Inside was a Christmas card and the words: *I do hope this will reach you on Christmas morning. Fondest love.* There was no signature or address. Both Mrs Baines and Constance burst into tears. Mrs Baines was still crying at dinner time when Samuel said, 'Now, Mother, you must cheer up, you know.'

'Yes, I must,' she said quickly. And she did.

Through Mrs Baines's influence, a new servant was found for Constance. Her name was Amy. She was a pretty girl, who had never worked as a servant before.

An hour before Mrs Baines's departure, Mr Povey came in with a poster.

'What is that, Samuel?' asked Mrs Baines.

'It's for our first Annual Sale,' replied Mr Povey, pretending that he was quite calm.

Mrs Baines hated sales. But she just frowned a little, and threw her head back in disgust. Constance was not present at this final defeat of the old ways.

## Surprises

One day, six years after their marriage, Mr Povey looked at his wife and said, quite suddenly, 'I shall be forty next birthday, you know!'

Constance was unpleasantly surprised. She knew, of course, that they were getting older, but it had never struck her before. She would be twenty-seven on her next birthday. Until recently, she had thought of a man of forty as nearly in his grave.

Trade in the shop was now excellent. Constance and Samuel were always busy. At long intervals, cards came from

Sophia, causing Constance more sorrow than joy. But the fact that she and Samuel understood and respected each other in their married life soon restored her sense of contentment.

Samuel was happy in his work and with his marriage, but he was still sometimes surprised at the way in which Constance reacted to things. Once he hinted that he did not much admire a new dress of hers. She never wore it again. After that, he was more careful about what he said.

Sometimes people asked them if they were sorry they had no children. They would answer that they really did not know what they would do if there was a baby. They had so much work to do at the shop...! They were quite sincere when they said this.

Then one day, there was an unexpected development in their lives.

One morning in March, a machine made of two equal-sized wooden wheels joined by a bar of iron, in the middle of which was a wooden saddle, appeared in St Luke's Square. It was a boneshaker—a kind of bicycle. Such a thing had never been seen there before.

It came from the shop of Samuel Povey's cousin Daniel, and was brought out by Daniel's son Dick, who was now eleven. Dick was a brave boy, and he enjoyed trying to ride the boneshaker around the square. After a little practice, he achieved a speed of almost six miles an hour!

The first time he came across the square, Samuel was standing outside the door of Baines's draper's shop. He stared at the boy on the boneshaker, his eyes wide with surprise.

The boy crashed into the pavement in front of him, and Samuel picked him up. He had not been hurt. But somehow, by picking the boy up, people felt that Samuel shared in the glory of this ride, and this made Samuel feel important.

5 Until then the cousins had not had much to do with each other, but this event changed that. Now they became friends.

Daniel was well known in Bursley. Everyone liked him. He was the leading baker, an officer at St Luke's church, and 10 a town councillor. He was a tall, handsome man, with a grey beard, an attractive smile, and dark flashing eyes. However, his marriage was not a happy one. He found it difficult to live at peace with his wife. She was lazy in the house, and would often make friends with other men.

15 One evening a few weeks later, Samuel had an even bigger surprise. Constance told him that she was pregnant. They looked at each other quickly like criminals who have discovered that they have set light to a bomb and cannot escape by running away. They looked at each other again and 20 again with a sweet, charming mixture of simple modesty and fearful joy.

Everything was changed. From then on, Samuel always did his best to help Constance meet what was coming to her.

## The baby

25 Two years later, Constance was standing at the sitting room window, looking out into the square. She was now almost twenty-nine, and her figure was rather heavier than it had been. She saw Samuel hurrying across the square towards the shop. She went down and opened the front door.

30 'Well?' she said.

'Mother's no better,' Samuel told her. 'In fact, she's worse. I should have stayed, only I knew you'd be worrying, so I caught the 3.50 train.'

'Did you see the doctor?' asked Constance.

35 'Yes.'

'What did he say?'

'Nothing much. When someone has reached that stage, you know—' answered Samuel.

Constance was back at the sitting room window. 'I don't like that cloud,' she murmured.

'What? Are they still out?' Samuel asked.

'Here they are!' cried Constance. She ran down the stairs again. A perambulator was being quickly pushed up the slope by a breathless girl.

'Oh, Amy,' Constance objected gently, 'I told you not to go far.'

'I hurried as fast as I could, madam, as soon as I saw it might rain.'

Constance put her arms into the perambulator and took from it the centre of her world. She ran into the house with him, although not a drop of rain had fallen yet. When she got to the sitting room, she sat down and hugged and kissed him before taking off his outdoor clothes.

'Here's Daddy!' she said.

Samuel came in. 'Oh, you little scoundrel!' he said gently, with a big proud smile on his face. 'Oh, you bad little fellow!' He put a finger out for the baby to hold.

The baby stared at the finger, and then looked into his father's face. He looked up at him with the most beautiful smile, and blew bubbles from his little mouth.

Samuel sat down and began to tell Constance the story of his trip. Mrs Baines, it seemed, having seen her grandson, was preparing to leave this world. She was worrying about Sophia, he said. Sophia had not written for a long time, and still no one knew her address. Mr Povey was feeling tired as he had had so much to do. He was busy in the shop, and he had been making frequent visits to Axe, too. Constance could not go herself at that time because of the baby.

Constance fed the baby sometimes at her breast and sometimes out of a bottle. Although Samuel always felt uncomfortable when he saw Constance feeding the baby at her breast, Constance herself never worried about it. It did mean, however, that she could not go on long journeys; she could not go as far as Axe.

For months before the baby had been born, Constance had wondered how it would affect their lives. Sometimes for a moment she was filled with terror at the thought of the birth itself. Then came the first pains—sharp, cruel warnings of even worse pains to come. The doctor was called. At first, Constance was apologetic, but then the real pains came thundering across her.

Someone put the twisted end of a towel in her hand. She pulled and pulled at it, so hard that she wondered why it did not break. And then she screamed. She felt that she was dying. She was terrified. And then came the last pressing down that never seemed to end, during which in her mind she said goodbye to herself ...

And then it was over. She found herself lying happily in bed, with the little soul that had fought its way out of her by her side. It did not look like a baby. It was red and wrinkled and creased. It did not even look human! Yet she felt an enormous tenderness for it.

Life was never the same after that. Miss Insull, the oldest of the young lady assistants, took over Constance's work in the shop. From that time, all Constance's time was given to looking after the baby.

One evening, when the baby had been placed in his cot for the night, she went down into the shop to see if there was anything she could do. Sam and Miss Insull were still working there, and Constance began to help them. After some time, Miss Insull said, 'Excuse me, I think I can hear the baby crying.'

'Let him cry,' said Mr Povey.

'I've made him perfectly comfortable,' said Constance. 'He's only crying because he thinks he's been left alone. We think he can't begin to learn too early.'

'How right you are,' said Miss Insull.

The noise went on for thirty minutes. Constance could not get on with her work. The crying went straight to her heart. Without saying a word, she crept upstairs.

After a moment, Mr Povey ran up after her. 'My dear,' he said to Constance, 'what are you going to do?'

'I'm just listening,' replied Constance.

'Do come down.'

'He may not be well.'

'Nonsense,' said Mr Povey impatiently.

They argued. The baby's cry rose to a scream. Constance would have walked through fire to go to him, but her husband's will held her back. Mr Povey himself felt angry and hurt that Constance would not return to the shop. It might have led to a quarrel if Miss Insull had not come running up the stairs.

'A telegram!' she said. 'The postmaster brought it himself. He said it was too late for normal delivery, but as it seemed important ...'

Samuel opened it and then looked serious, and sad. He gave it to his wife. Tears came to her eyes. Mrs Baines had died.

'I'll get Cousin Daniel to drive me over at once,' Samuel said. In less than a minute, he had gone.

Constance ran upstairs again, but the crying had stopped. She turned the door knob softly, slowly, and crept into the room. A night light made large shadows around the cot. Constance held up the light, and looked down at her little son. Yes, he had decided to fall asleep. A death far away had just defeated his obstinate little heart. Fate had got the better of him. How amazingly soft that tear-stained little cheek looked; how delicate the little hands appeared. The baby slept. In Constance, grief for her mother was strangely united with joy in her child. It was a riddle she did not completely understand, and yet she accepted it.

# 5
# Cyril

## The cake

The little boy's name was Samuel Cyril Povey; everyone called him Cyril. From the day he was born, he immediately became the most important person in the house. Everything that was done there was done for him. His father was always teaching him to consider his mother, and she was always teaching him to consider his father, but he was not deceived. He knew that he was the most important person in the whole town.

At four and a half years old, he was dark-haired like his father, handsome like his aunt, tall for his age, and clever. There was nothing that he could not say, he could walk and run, and he was full of exact knowledge about everything around him.

One afternoon, there was a children's party at the house for him and his little friends. He was talking about his picture books to a pretty little four-year-old girl called Jennie when something happened.

One of the adults at the party began to pass round a brown cake with white sugar and red balls on it. It was quite an ordinary cake, but it was the cake that Cyril loved more than any other. The other children liked it too.

One little boy took two pieces. The lady who was passing the cake round objected, and began telling the little boy off. At once Constance and Samuel came over. They smiled and said that it was quite all right for the little fellow to have two pieces if that was what he wanted.

All this talk attracted Cyril's attention, and he noticed for the first time that his favourite cake was being handed round. He saw that it was almost all gone. When the lady persuaded Jennie to take the last piece, and there was none left for him, Cyril gave a despairing shout. He began to cry. He turned on Jennie, sobbing, and tried to take her piece of cake. Jennie was not used to such outrageous behaviour. She defended her property. Cyril hit her in the eye, took the piece of cake and tried to push it all into his mouth at once. It was too big for him to swallow. Pieces of cake and tears mixed together around his mouth and all over his face. The mess was terrible. Jennie wept loudly.

Constance picked Cyril up and took him to his room. There she smacked him and told him he was a naughty boy. She took the cake out of his mouth, wiped his face, and left him upstairs. Jennie was still crying when Constance returned to the party, and it was decided that she should go home. Everybody pretended that it was nothing. Such things, they said, were always happening at children's parties.

When the party was over and all the children had left, Samuel said to Constance, 'I thought you said that the boy was in his bedroom. He isn't.'

Constance went to the door of the sitting room and called out, 'Amy! Is Cyril with you?'

'No, madam. He was here a short time ago, but then I told him to go upstairs.'

For a moment, Samuel and Constance thought nothing of it. Then, a few moments later, the idea entered both their heads that Cyril might have gone out of the house. They ran down to the kitchen together and questioned Amy. In tears, Amy admitted that she had left Cyril alone in the kitchen for some minutes, and that the side door of the house had been open. All three of them searched through every room of the house. No Cyril. They were all very worried. The two women returned to the sitting room, not quite knowing where to look next. Amy was crying.

'There's no use you standing there sobbing, Amy,' Constance said. 'He'll be found soon. He can't have gone far. Mr Povey is still looking around for him.'

Soon afterwards, Samuel came in. He was carrying a black mass in his arms. It was Cyril. Constance gave a scream when she saw how dirty he was. 'Where ever did you find him?' she asked.

'In the cellar. He was with me when I was working down there yesterday. I suddenly thought that that is where he might have gone.'

'I'll take him,' said Constance. 'He will have to go in the bath.'

'No, I'll look after him,' said Samuel severely. He carried the little boy upstairs. When Constance tried to follow, he made her go down again, which she did, weeping.

An hour later, Mr Povey came down. 'He's in bed now,' he said.

'But have you washed him?' Constance asked, tears coming to her eyes.

'I've washed him.'

'But what have you done to him?' Constance sobbed.

'I've punished him, of course,' her husband replied. 'What did you expect me to do? Someone had to do it.'


## School

At nine, Cyril was large and heavy for a boy of his age. He had a round face and short hair.

One cold morning, not long after Easter, he was standing in the kitchen by the fire, trying to make it burn brighter. It was about five minutes to eight.

'Now, Master Cyril,' Amy objected, 'leave that fire alone, will you?'

'Shut up, Amy, or I'll hit you in the eye,' the boy answered.

'You ought to be ashamed of yourself!' said Amy.

'Oh, go to hell!'

'I'll tell your mother!'

Cyril was perfectly sure that she would not tell his mother. And yet, what if she did? Cyril felt uncomfortable, but hid his feelings by laughing.

'You wouldn't!' he shouted.

'Wouldn't I? You'll see. As soon as I see your mother next …!'

But when Constance arrived, Amy said nothing. Cyril was

saved once more. He said to himself that never again would he let his soul be disturbed by any threats from old Amy.

That morning, Cyril was to go to a new school—a real school for boys, not one where there were girls, too. He was looking forward to it.

At breakfast, his father, now fifty and quite fat, said, 'There's one thing you must always remember, my boy. Never be late either in going to school or in coming home. And so that you may have no excuse, here's something for you.'

It was a silver watch and chain.

Cyril was surprised. So was Constance. Samuel had said nothing to her about giving Cyril the watch.

Samuel took Cyril to the new school. When Cyril came home that afternoon, he was highly excited and very pleased with himself. He had been put in the third form. He would soon be at the top of it, he said. He loved the school, and the other boys liked him.

That night, in bed, when Samuel and Constance discussed their son, Constance was glad to learn that her husband had no intention of making him work in the shop when he grew up. Cyril would become a doctor or a lawyer!

Cyril loved school. He seemed to be made for it. By the end of the summer term, he was top of his form. He won one of the few prizes—a box of drawing instruments—given out at the school speech day. When his parents visited, they were shown a beautiful map that he had drawn and coloured. It was on display in the school hall. They were both very proud of him.

Cyril was good at drawing, and he was interested in art. He would have liked to have studied the subject, but it was not taught at school. He would have had to go out one evening a week to the School of Art, and Samuel would not allow him to go out alone in the evening. This also affected another of Cyril's interests. He was good at games, and he wanted to go to the playing fields in the evening to practise. His father agreed to take him, but after going once, Cyril refused to go again. The other boys had seen his father bring him and wait for him until it was time to go home. They had accused Cyril of being a baby.

# A liar and a thief

As he grew older, although successful at school, Cyril became less and less easy to live with at home. He was rough. He often shouted and whistled in the house. When he moved
5  about, he was clumsy and noisy. He frequently forgot to say 'Please' when he asked for things. He replied impatiently to polite questions, or he did not reply at all until the questions were repeated. His shoelaces were often undone or in knots, his fingernails were always dirty, his hair was always
10  untidy—he would rather die than put oil on it. His appetite was larger than his mother thought could be possible. It had to be admitted that Cyril was no longer the nice little boy he used to be. But all the same, he was a good boy, Constance would often say to herself, and now and then she said it to
15  Samuel.

One day, when Cyril was thirteen, the headmaster came to the shop. He talked to Mr Povey quietly and seriously for about a quarter of an hour. After Mr Povey had taken him to the door, he returned, looking rather angry. He said
20  nothing to Constance or Cyril, but asked Amy some sharp questions. They went down to the cellar together. Amy was weeping when she returned, but had been told to say nothing.

Just after Cyril had left for school one morning a few days
25  later, his father ran out of the house after him.

'Come back home, please, Cyril,' he said.

They returned together, and went into the sitting room. Constance was there, doing some work. She was surprised to see both her husband and her son coming back into the house
30  at that time. However, she could see from the look on her husband's face that something serious was in the air, so she said nothing.

'What money have you got in your pockets?' Samuel asked the boy.

35  'One and a half pence,' Cyril murmured, looking down at the floor.

'Where did you get it from?' asked Mr Povey.

'It's part of what Mother gave me,' answered Cyril.

'I did give him three pence last week,' Constance said.

'Is that all you've got?' said Mr Povey to the boy.

'Yes, Father,' the boy replied.

'Empty your pockets,' said the father.

Cyril did so, and a silver two-shilling coin appeared.

'Give that to your mother, please,' said Mr Povey.

When Constance had taken it, Mr Povey said, 'Is there a cross on it?'

Constance was crying, and she had to wipe her eyes. Then she said, 'Yes.'

'Where did you get it from?' asked Mr Povey.

'Out of the cash drawer in the shop,' replied Cyril.

'Have you ever taken anything out of that drawer before?' asked the father.

'Yes,' replied Cyril.                                                    20

'And how have you been spending this money?' asked Mr Povey, looking right into his son's eyes.

'On sweets,' Cyril replied.

'Well, now you can go down to the cellar and bring back that little box of yours. You know the one I mean.'      25

Cyril went, and while he was out of the room, Samuel explained things to Constance. A lot of boys at the school had been caught smoking; but what had worried the headmaster much more than this was that some of the boys

had bought themselves expensive pipes and cigarette holders. The headmaster wondered where they had got the money to pay for them. He thought one of the boys must be stealing money from home. He had spoken to all the parents
5 of these boys secretly, and warned them.

Mr Povey had discovered from Amy that Cyril had a store of things in the cellar—a pipe, some tobacco, a cigar and a packet of cheap cigarettes. Cyril said his friends had given them to him, but that was not true. Mr Povey had also marked
10 every silver coin in the shop till; the two-shilling coin found in Cyril's pocket had obviously come from there.

When Cyril returned with the box, he showed no signs of being sorry. He said he thought it was unfair that his father never gave him any money. Mr Povey called his son a liar
15 and a thief. They were both angry with each other.

'He's to have nothing but bread and water,' Mr Povey said to Constance, after he had sent Cyril up to his room.

Later that day, Constance told her husband she had been up to talk to Cyril, and that he had wept for what he had
20 done. Mr Povey seemed satisfied. But all three of them, and Amy too, felt that life could never be the same again after that.


## Another crime

One night, six months after the tragedy of the two-shilling
25 coin, Samuel Povey was woken up by a hand on his shoulder. 'Father!' a voice whispered. Samuel sat up.

'Someone is throwing dirt or something at our windows,' Cyril said.

Sure enough, Samuel could hear things hitting his
30 window. Carefully he opened it and looked out. A man was standing outside in the square.

'Is that you, Samuel?' came a low voice.

'Yes,' Samuel answered cautiously. 'Is that Cousin Daniel?'

'I want you,' said Daniel.

35 Samuel sent Cyril back to his bedroom, and then dressed and went downstairs. When he opened the side door, he

could see Daniel signalling to him at the corner of the square. Samuel ran across to him, but Daniel did not wait. He turned and went into his shop. Samuel followed as quickly as he could.

As soon as Samuel was inside his cousin's shop, Daniel shut the door quickly and locked it. The suddenness of the movement quite startled Samuel.

'Is anything wrong, Daniel?' he asked.

'You know that my wife drinks,' said Daniel, looking hard at Samuel.

'No,' said Samuel. 'No one's ever said—'

'She drinks,' Daniel continued, 'and she's done so for the past two years.'

'I'm sorry to hear it,' Samuel answered.

'I wish that was the worst,' Daniel murmured.

Samuel was beginning to get worried.

'I went to Liverpool today, and when I got back, I found Dick sitting on the stairs in the dark almost naked. He had been in bed all day with a feverish cold, but my wife hadn't gone up to see him. The whole day he hadn't had anything to eat. Late this afternoon, he came down to see what was happening. He slipped on the stairs and broke his knee or twisted it or something. He sat there for hours, unable to move.'

'And your wife—?' asked Samuel.

'She was in the sitting room the whole time—completely drunk! I helped Dick get back upstairs to his bedroom. Here! Come here!' He took Samuel to the bottom of the stairs, and then said, 'Listen!'

The noises coming from Dick's bedroom sounded more like the cries of a child than those of a young man in his twenties.

'That's Dick!' said Daniel.

'But he must be in terrible pain! Haven't you fetched the doctor?'

'Not yet.'

Samuel stared at his cousin for a second. Daniel looked old and helpless. 'He's losing his mind,' Samuel thought.

'I must take charge here.' Then he said to Daniel, 'I'll just run upstairs and look at him.'

Dick's bedroom was very untidy, and it looked as if it had not been cleaned for a long time.

'Is that you, Doctor?' came a voice from the bed.

'He's coming,' said Samuel gently.

'Well, if he doesn't get here soon, I'll be dead before he arrives,' said Dick, weak but angry.

Samuel ran downstairs. 'Daniel,' he said, 'this is really silly. Why didn't you fetch the doctor while you were waiting for me? Where's your wife?'

'You'd better go and look at her. She's still in the sitting room.'

Samuel went in, afraid of what he might find.

The sitting room was as untidy and dirty as Dick's bedroom. Mrs Daniel Povey was lying awkwardly on an old sofa, her head back, her face pale, her eyes swollen, and her mouth wet and wide open. She was quite still. It was a horribly nasty sight. Samuel was frightened and disgusted.

'But—' he stammered.

'Yes, Samuel,' said Daniel. 'I think I've killed her! I shook her and took her by the neck, and before I knew what had happened, she had suffocated. I didn't mean to strangle her, you know, I just …'

Samuel felt as if someone had given him an unimaginably violent blow. His heart shivered.

Dick's cries could still be heard coming from upstairs. 'I'll fetch the doctor,' Samuel said.

When Samuel returned with the doctor, Daniel was    5
standing at the door of his shop, talking to a policeman. The policeman was in a high state of excitement. He knew that Daniel Povey was an important tradesman and a town councillor, and it seemed that he had killed his wife. The policeman had never known such a thing to happen before—    10
not at any rate in Bursley.

Half an hour later, Samuel left Daniel at the police station and went to fetch Constance. He told her what had happened, and asked her to look after Dick until he could be taken to the hospital.    15

The following morning, a crowd of at least 200 people gathered in St Luke's Square. They stood about in the November mud, staring at Daniel Povey's shop. There was nothing to be seen. The body of Mrs Povey had already been taken away, young Dick Povey was on his way to hospital,    20
and Daniel Povey was under arrest at the police station. But the crowd continued to wait there. What had happened was both startling and special. It seemed right that it should be spoken about and thought over. Complete strangers discussed the events of the night before with one another.    25

Samuel came out of his house and hurried to the home of young Lawton, son of the late 'Lawyer Lawton'. The two men then drove to the police station together. There, a crowd as big as the one outside Daniel Povey's shop had collected. The arrival of Samuel and the lawyer's son caused great    30
excitement.

The same day, Daniel appeared before the local court. He was accused of murdering his wife, and then taken back to the police station. He would remain there for some weeks, until he could be tried in the higher court at Stafford.    35

# 6
# The Widow

## The trial

When the day of Daniel Povey's trial came, Samuel went to Stafford, even though he was not feeling well. He had a bad cold. A few days in bed, or even just sitting in a warm room, would have cured it, but he could not stay still in one place for any length of time. He was too worried. He would not listen to anything Constance said to him. His mind was elsewhere. It was as if he were in a dream.

At last, Constance stopped being her usual soft, gentle, agreeable self. She screamed at Samuel, accusing him of thinking more about his cousin than his own wife and son. But it was all useless. Samuel just answered coldly that he would do what he thought was right.

Constance was sure he was putting his life in danger. She could see that his only thoughts were of trying to save his cousin from being hanged. The next morning, she heard him leave the house very early and go out into the cold winter darkness. For some time she could hear his terrible cough as he walked away to the station.

That afternoon, Constance was working in the shop when Mr Critchlow came in. He was holding a newspaper. 'It's begun!' he said, referring to the trial. In a strange way, he seemed happy.

Constance was more worried about her husband's health than about what might happen to Daniel Povey; however, she was still interested. 'I hope everything will be all right,' she murmured.

'Everything will be all right,' Mr Critchlow said happily. 'Only it will be all wrong for Daniel Povey.' He spoke loudly so that all the assistants in the shop could hear him. 'People in the town say that he never meant to kill his wife. But that's not a good argument against hanging a man. Then I'm told that she used to get drunk, and that she never cleaned her house. But I don't see any judge telling a jury that men can punish their wives for such things by strangling them. He did wrong, and he deserves to be punished for it.'

'I'm surprised at you, Mr Critchlow! I really am!' Constance said sharply. She was horrified and angry to see someone so pleased at another's misfortune.

Later that day, Constance looked through an evening paper for the latest news about the trial. The jury had found Daniel guilty, but had recommended mercy. The judge said he would pass on the jury's recommendation; but at the same time, he sentenced Daniel to be hanged. There was now only a small chance that Daniel might be reprieved.

Constance and Cyril waited until late that night for Samuel to return. When he got home, the dreadful condition of his mind and his body terrified his wife. His cold and cough were much worse. Amy and Cyril took him up to bed. 'If he hasn't recovered by tomorrow, I shall send for the doctor!' Constance said. She swore she would keep him there by force if necessary.

## The petition

The next morning, Samuel seemed much better, but when young Lawton came to see him about Daniel, Constance insisted on their talking in the bedroom.

The two men decided to send a petition to the government minister in charge of executions—the Home Secretary. News of this quickly spread around. Within days, there was an angry demand from thousands of people for a reprieve for Daniel Povey. Hundreds of forms for signatures were printed, and in the end, nearly 25,000 people signed to say they supported the petition. The petition and signatures were taken to London and handed to the Home Secretary.

During this time, Samuel worked hard on the petition, and his health improved. Although it was the middle of winter, and the weather was often cold and wet, nothing would stop him from going out to get signatures. His cough did not go away, but it was nowhere near as bad as it had been.

The petition, however, did not succeed. The Home Secretary said Daniel's sentence of death must go ahead—he would not be reprieved.

The flame of Samuel Povey's hopes died when the petition failed. The day that he went to Stafford to see his cousin for the last time, his mind seemed to be fixed on the execution. He could think of nothing else. He returned in a state of near madness. He talked about what he had seen. When he came to the point where Dick, who was still in hospital, had had to be brought to the prison especially to see his father for the last time, he wept without being able to stop.

The following morning, the local newspaper told its readers what Daniel Povey had had for his last breakfast and the exact length of the rope with which he had been hanged.

Later that day, Constance and Cyril were standing at the sitting room window looking out into the square.

'Oh, Mother!' Cyril exclaimed suddenly. 'Listen! I'm sure I can hear the band.'

He was right. Two town bands were approaching, playing the 'Death March'.

Each of the members of the bands had in his hat a card with a black edge all the way round it. The cards said:

*DANIEL POVEY*
*A COUNCILLOR OF THIS TOWN*
*MURDERED BY THE LAW THIS MORNING*
*8 FEBRUARY 1888*
*'HE WAS MORE SINNED AGAINST THAN SINNING'*

The streets of Bursley were crowded with people protesting against something they considered cruelly unjust. For a while, the people stood in the square and listened to the speeches that were made. After that, they returned sadly to their homes.

Winter was nearly over, but the weather was still bad. The temperature fell, icy rain swept across the town, and Samuel's cough got worse. His face looked red and hot; he was beginning to have a fever; and he was breathing fast. When he coughed, pain shot through his body, and he put his hand to his side. He refused to eat anything, and that badly frightened Constance. She asked Cyril to fetch the doctor.

'It sounds like pneumonia,' said the doctor when he arrived.

During the three worst months of the year, Samuel had escaped the dangers of a man who goes out in all kinds of weather even though he has a bad cough. That last journey to Stafford, however, had been one journey too many. Less than a week later, Samuel Povey was dead.

## Giving way

On the first Monday after Samuel's funeral, work went on as usual in the shop. Constance faced her husband's death with calmness. She did not feel that her life was at an end. She had Cyril to think about.

In the afternoon, she left him doing his homework and went down to the shop. What was she to do with the business, she wondered? Keep it or sell it? She was a rich woman, with the money her parents and her aunt had left her, so she did not need to keep the shop. But leaving it would break old habits, and she would have to find a new home. She did not like the idea of doing that. If she wanted to keep the business going, she knew that Miss Insull would help her.

When the shop had been closed for the night, she went back to the sitting room. Cyril was drawing a picture.

'Have you finished your lessons?' Constance said.

Cyril replied, without thinking much about it, 'Yes.' Then after a pause he added, 'Except my arithmetic. I shall do that in the morning before breakfast.'

'Oh, Cyril!' she complained.

5  It had been a rule for a long time that there was to be no drawing before lessons were done. While his father was alive, Cyril never dared to break it.

Cyril went on drawing. Constance wanted to order him to go on with his lessons, but she could not. She feared an
10  argument. She mistrusted herself. She felt sad that she had to face a challenge from her son, and so soon after his father's death!

'You know you won't have time tomorrow morning!' she said feebly.

15  'Oh, Mother!' he answered in a superior voice. 'Don't worry.'

She sighed and sat down.

Soon Amy came to lay the supper. 'Now, Master Cyril,' she announced sharply, 'let me have the table, please!'

20  'What a nuisance you are, Amy!' he answered rudely. 'Look, Mother, can't Amy put the cloth on half the table? I'm right in the middle of my drawing.'

Constance said quickly, 'All right, Amy. Just this once.'

Amy obeyed unwillingly.

25  Cyril ate his supper quickly and then got out his colours.

'You surely aren't thinking of beginning to paint that at this time of the night!' Constance said, astonished.

'Oh, yes, Mother!' he said in a complaining voice. 'It isn't late.'

30  Another rule of his father's had been that there should be nothing after supper except bed. Nine o'clock was the latest time allowed for going to bed. It was now less than a quarter to.

'Now, Cyril,' Constance said, 'I do hope you are going to
35  be a good boy and not cause me any anxiety.'

But she said it too kindly.

He said sullenly, 'I do think you might let me finish it. I've begun it. It won't take me long.'

'It mustn't occur again,' Constance said.

The clock struck nine, and it struck half past nine. At ten minutes to ten, she said, 'Now, Cyril, when the clock strikes ten, I shall really put the light out.'

The clock struck ten. She stood up and put her hand to the gaslight.

'Half a moment!' he cried. 'I've finished!'

Her hand stopped.

Another four minutes passed and then he jumped up. 'There!' he said proudly, showing her his picture.

'Yes, it's good,' Constance commented without much interest.

'I don't believe you care for it!' he accused her.

'I care for your health. Just look at that clock!'

He sat down again deliberately.

'Now, Cyril!'

'Well, Mother, I suppose you'll let me take my boots off!' he said teasingly.

During the next few days, Constance was less worried about Cyril. He did not try to repeat his naughty behaviour. In fact, as if by a miracle, he had got up early on Tuesday morning and done his arithmetic.

And then, on the Friday of the following week, he was late! He came in with his clothes covered with mud. He had been playing football. Constance sent him to wash before his tea. She expected him to say he was sorry for being late when he returned, but he just sat down at the table without apologizing. In fact, he behaved rudely and noisily during the meal, and before it was finished, he said suddenly, 'You'll just have to let me go to the School of Art after Easter, you know.' He stared at her with a fixed challenge in his eyes.

He meant evening classes at the School of Art. His father had been against it.

'You remember what your father said,' Constance replied.

'But, Mother, the drawing master says that if I'm going to take up drawing, I ought to start at once, and I suppose he ought to know.'

'I can't allow you to do it yet,' said Constance quietly.

He frowned at her sullenly, and then he sulked. It was war between them.

He went on arguing for days after that, behaving like his Aunt Sophia had so many years previously. He stopped drawing entirely.

After several weeks of unhappiness, Constance asked, 'How many evenings do you want to go each week?'

The war was over.

He was charming again. Constance said to herself, 'If we can be happy together only when I let him have his way, then I shall just have to surrender.' She comforted herself with such thoughts on three evenings a week as she sat alone, waiting for him to return.

## The new landlord

In the summer of that year, a rich citizen of Bursley, who had owned the Baines shop and the Critchlow shop among many other buildings, died. The Baines family had been paying him rent for many years, but now their shop and all the others were to be sold by auction.

Mr Critchlow came to see Constance as soon as he heard the news. He asked her if she planned to buy her shop.

'Not me!' she answered. 'I've got quite enough house property already.'

She took Cyril with her to the auction. The bids for the Baines house and shop began at 1,000 pounds and went up slowly. Mr Critchlow made the final bid of 1,550 pounds, and the shop was his. He also bought his own.

Constance hated the idea of having Mr Critchlow as her landlord, but she also did not want to leave the only home she had ever known.

On Thursday afternoon of the same week, Mr Critchlow came to see her. Miss Insull was in the shop at the time.

'Well, Mrs Povey,' he began mysteriously, 'we've made it up between us. No doubt some people will say we have taken a long time about it, but I don't think that that is any business of theirs.'

Constance stared at him, not knowing what he was talking about.

'What ...?' she began.

'Me and her!' He nodded in the direction of Miss Insull, who was now standing at the back of the shop with an odd look on her face.

Constance was astonished; Mr Critchlow and Miss Insull, it seemed, were engaged to be married! As far as Constance could tell, Miss Insull was forty years old. Mr Critchlow was a widower, and much older; his wife had died before Miss Insull was born.

'I am sure I congratulate you both,' Constance breathed. 'I am sure I hope you will be happy.'

'We'll be all right,' said Mr Critchlow.

'Thank you, Mrs Povey,' said Maria Insull.

For a moment, all three were silent, not knowing what to say next. Then Mr Critchlow remarked that he would like to buy the draper's business from Constance. Miss Insull—or Mrs Critchlow as she would soon be—would manage it, and Mr Critchlow would continue to work in his chemist's shop.

Constance was still not happy. She did not mind selling the business, but she did not want to lose her home. Mr Critchlow then made her a proposal. 'We'll divide the shop from the house,' he suggested, 'and you can continue to have the house. The whole thing was two houses anyway before they were joined to make the shop and the house.'

Constance thought about it for a few days, and finally she agreed.

The job of dividing the house from the shop took a long time, and the workers made a terrible mess, but in the end it was all done.

## Cyril's ambition

5 In 1893 there lived at No 4 St Luke's Square a new and strange young man. The untidy, noisy boy Cyril had gone, never to return. In his place was a new Cyril, smart, handsome, clean, polite, and always dressed in the latest fashion. Although he had been big and clumsy as a child, as a
10 man he was slim, elegant, and no taller or fatter than most other young men. His mother could hardly recognize him. She was immensely proud of him, even though she only saw him at meals. During the day, he worked in the art department at 'Peels', an important manufacturer of pottery.
15 Every evening he studied at the School of Art.

Constance found him difficult to please, not because he was demanding, but because he was not interested in anything but his work and his art. He had no bad habits. He was always charming and kind, except when Constance
20 mistakenly tried to stop him from doing what he wanted. He never noticed anything that she did, and she never got over the hope that he would.

Then, on a hot day in August, just before they were to go off for a month's holiday in the Isle of Man, Cyril came home
25 and said, 'Well, Mother, I've got it.' He spoke with careful calm, looking up at the ceiling.

'Got what?' asked Constance.

'The National Scholarship,' said Cyril.

'What's that?' asked Constance.

30 'Now, Mother,' he warned her, 'don't go and say I've never mentioned it!' He felt rather nervous, and he could see that she was highly disturbed by what he had just told her.

Never, in fact—not even by the death of her husband— had Constance received such a frightful blow as Cyril had
35 just given her. It did not come as a complete surprise, however. About three months previously, he had certainly

mentioned a National Scholarship, and he had said that such a thing would mean studying and living in London. But he had made it seem so unlikely that she had not been worried.

And now it seemed there was nothing she could do. She knew that it would be as much use asking for mercy from a 5 tiger as from her good, hard-working son.

'I shall get free lessons and money to live on,' Cyril said.

'For how long?' she managed to ask.

'Well, at first for a year. But if I work hard, it will be continued for three years,' Cyril answered. 10

She knew that if he stayed away for three years, he would never come back.

For a moment, she held on to a slight hope. He could not leave her without her agreement because he was under twenty-one. And he would need a lot more money, which he 15 could get only from her. She could refuse ... but no! She could not refuse. He was the master, the king. For the sake of a pleasant life, she had weakly given way to him from the start! He was spoilt, and there was nothing she could do about it now. 20

'You don't seem very happy about it, Mother!' he said.

She went out of the room. He had tried to be gentle, but his joy at the chance of leaving Bursley was too great for him to hide, and too much for her to bear.

The holiday on the Isle of Man was of course ruined. 25 Constance thought of nothing but the fact that Cyril would soon be leaving home. She could hardly walk because of the heavy weight that she carried in her heart.

On returning home, after she had gone to the station with him to say goodbye, she argued irritably with her soul, 'After 30 all, could you expect the boy to do anything else? He is a serious student. He has been very successful. Do you expect him to be tied to you forever?'

But sadly, her soul kept on repeating, 'I'm a lonely old woman now. I have nothing to live for any more.' 35

# 7
# The Elopement

### Lovers' quarrel

Sophia was waiting for Gerald Scales in her room at the
Hatfield Hotel, in London. It was the afternoon of 1 July
1866.

5   There was a knock at the door. 'He's nearly as nervous as I
am!' she thought. She coughed. The moment had now come
which would divide her life as a battle divides the history of
a nation.

Her mind swept backwards through the last unbelievable
10   three months. The tricks she had had to play to get and hide
Gerald's letters at the shop, and to reply to them! The far
more complicated and dangerous tricks she had played on
her Aunt Harriet! The visits to the post office at Axe! The
three wonderful meetings with Gerald in the early morning
15   by the canal, when he had told her of the money he had been
left by his aunt and the unkindness of his uncle Boldero, and
then his offer to her of a chance of everlasting happiness! The
nights of fear! The daring departure from her aunt's house!
The terrible lies she had told about visiting her sick mother!
20   The awful moment of meeting Gerald when he got onto the
train at Rugby! Who was this bold, mad Sophia? Surely not
herself!

The knock at the door was impatiently repeated.

'Come in,' she said in a timid voice.

25   Gerald entered the room. He, the retired travelling sales
representative of Birkinshaws, who had been everywhere and
through everything, was highly nervous, too. He had taken
the room for Sophia only for the day, intending to continue
their journey that evening. He walked in and kissed her
30   lovingly.

Sophia kissed him back even more passionately. 'I've
got nobody but you now,' she murmured softly and
sweetly.

She thought that these words would please him. She did not realize that they would put him off. They would remind him of his responsibilities rather than his rights. He smiled rather weakly. A less innocent girl would have seen from that smile that she could do anything with Gerald except trust him. But Sophia still had to learn.

'Are you ready?' he asked.

'Yes,' she answered.

'Well, would you like to go and see the new pictures in the National Gallery?' he asked again.

'But what about the—wedding?' she said in a whisper.

'Oh,' he said lightly and quickly, 'I was just going to tell you. It can't be done here. There's been some change in the rules; I only found out last night. We can get the British Consul in Paris to marry us quite easily, and as I've got the boat tickets for us to go across tonight, as we arranged ...'

She sat down suddenly, feeling terribly shocked. She believed what he said. She did not suspect that he was using the old trick of men who try to cheat girls. It was his tone that shocked her. It suggested that marriage was of no great importance. Had it really been his intention to set off on a journey and only mention later, 'Oh, we can't be married at half past two today as I told you'? She was astonished that he thought she was so stupid! He must himself be stupid in some ways not to realize how enormous her sacrifice had been in running away with him even as far as London. She felt sorry for him.

'It'll be all right!' Gerald tried to persuade her.

'Oh, no!' she answered sharply. 'Oh, no! We can't possibly go like that. You should have told me before.'

'But how could I?' he complained. For a moment, he really believed that it was a change in the rules that had prevented him from carrying out his honourable purpose. The truth was that he had done absolutely nothing about making any arrangements.

He touched the back of her neck with his lips, and she jumped up, sobbing and angry. 'Please do not touch me!' she reacted fiercely.

'Then what are you going to do?' he asked in a tone that combined scorn with cruelty. She was making a fool of him and he did not like it.

'I can tell you what I shan't do. I shan't go to Paris,' said Sophia.

'That isn't my question. I want to know what you will do,' said Gerald.

'What's that got to do with you?' asked Sophia.

'It's got everything to do with me.'

'Well, you can go, and then you will find out!' said Sophia.

He was at heart a coward, and that urged him to take advantage of her words. 'Well, then, goodbye,' he said, turning towards the door.

'I suppose you'd leave me here without any money or anything?' she said icily. Her sneer was more destructive than his. It destroyed in him the last bit of pity for her.

'Oh, I'm so sorry!' he said coldly, and counted out five one-pound coins.

'Do you think I'd take your dirty money?' she asked defiantly.

At first, she wanted to throw the coins in his face, but she paused, and then threw them deliberately on the floor.

'Pick them up!' she commanded.

'No, thanks,' he said, and left shutting the door behind him.

Sophia sat down on the bed. 'I've been a wicked girl,' she said to herself severely, wondering what she was going to do.

She would not go back to Bursley or Axe. She could not because she had stolen money from Aunt Harriet—as much as she had thrown back at Gerald. She was happy she had taken it, for without it she would not have been able to repulse Gerald with that sneer. But it meant that as a thief, she could never look her mother in the face again without feeling ashamed of herself.

Actually, Aunt Harriet did discover the loss, but said nothing about it to anyone. She knew it would have been cruel to Sophia's mother.

Now Sophia had no idea what she should do. Although she was often arrogant and audacious, she had never really been out in the world on her own before. She felt as helpless as a rabbit. The very idea of going out of her room made her nervous. She went to the window, pulled the curtain aside  5 and looked out. She could see the river. 'I suppose I could go down there tonight and drown myself,' she thought. 'A nice thing that would be for Gerald!'

Then she turned, and throwing herself back onto the bed, quietly wept.  10

## A change of heart

Gerald Scales walked along the London streets with no clear idea about where he was going. He was wondering what his uncle would say if he knew that he had tried to persuade a girl to elope with him. His offer to Sophia of marriage in front  15 of the British Consul in Paris was, of course, just so much nonsense. Once there, he had hoped to be able to take advantage of her—to make her his mistress.

However, that was all over now; he had got out of it. It was silly to think that Sophia would ever have been right for  20 him. She had nearly made a fool of him. He had kept his dignity, he said to himself; but all the time his dignity and his pride were suffering.

'Oh, hell!' he murmured at last. 'I suppose I must go through with it.' He was desperate. He was ready to pay any  25 price to be able to say to himself that he had done what he had set his heart on doing. He went back to the hotel. He wondered if Sophia might have gone, and the fear of that already made him feel sick.

When he entered her room, he saw her lying face down on  30 the bed. Her hat was on the floor. This sight seemed to him to be the most touching he had ever seen. He forgot everything except the deep, strange emotion that affected him at this time. He approached the bed. She did not move.

Having heard someone come in, and knowing that it must  35 be Gerald, Sophia forced herself to remain still. A wild,

splendid hope shot up in her. But she could not control the
sob that had been waiting in her throat.

The sound of the sob brought tears to Gerald's eyes.

'Sophia,' he whispered.

5 But she did not stir. Another sob shook her.

'All right, then. We'll stay in London till we can be married.'
A silence.

'Thank you!' she wept. 'Thank you!'

He saw that her little hand was moving out towards his.

10 He seized it, and knelt down by the bed and put his arm
round her waist. An immense relief went slowly through
them both.

'I really couldn't have gone to Paris without being
married,' she said at last.

15 'No, no!' he said gently. 'Of course you couldn't. It was I
who was wrong.'

She sat up and kissed him. Everything was right again
now. Everything was forgotten. For Gerald, she was again the
mistress he had hoped for. Now, however, she would also be

20 his wife.

He found a church and a priest near the hotel, and
preparations were made for the wedding. So as not to hurt
him, she did not mention the changed rules that he had
previously said prevented them from getting married in

25 London. A day after their marriage, she sent the telegram to
her mother.

## Paris

Three months had passed. Sophia and Gerald were returning
to Paris after having had lunch outside the city, at Versailles.

30 As they came to the centre of Paris, their taxi passed a
splendid carriage with a lady sitting alone in the back.

'My God!' Gerald said suddenly. 'That's Hortense! Look—
in that carriage.'

'Hortense?' Sophia asked simply.

35 'Yes, Hortense Schneider.'

'Who is she?' Sophia asked again.

'You've never heard of Hortense Schneider?'

'No!'

'Well, have you heard of Offenbach?' Gerald asked impatiently.

'I don't think so.'

He seemed unable to believe it. 'Haven't you heard of *Bluebeard*?'

'Of course. Who hasn't?'                                           10

'I mean the opera, by Offenbach.'

She shook her head, hardly knowing even what an opera was.

'Well, well! Whatever next?' he said, completely astonished that anyone could possibly know so little.   15
Actually he was delighted that he had such a simple person to teach and manoeuvre. As for Sophia, she was always happy to learn from him, and for the moment she liked to pretend she was a little ignorant know-nothing.

That evening, they went to a famous restaurant. It was   20
after midnight when they arrived. Some of the women there were prostitutes, out for the evening with their men friends.

They had bright red lips, powder on their cheeks, cold, hard eyes, and arrogant faces. Sophia's face, so childlike and trusting, so confident of its pure beauty, looked entirely different.

5 Sophia could not understand the bold behaviour of these women. They, on the other hand, saw nothing in Sophia they envied, except for her youth.

Gerald loudly gave orders to the head waiter in French, and they sat down. When their soup and wine arrived, 10 Sophia began to give Gerald her opinion of the other women's clothes. She soon realized that he was getting tired of listening to her, so she stopped.

'What do you think they are talking about?' Gerald said, indicating by a movement of his head the group of men and 15 women at the next table.

'What?' Sophia asked.

'The execution of a murderer called Rivain the day after tomorrow. They're arranging to go and see it,' replied Gerald.

'Oh, what a horrible idea!'

'They'll use the guillotine, you know!' said Gerald.

'But can people see it?'

'Yes, of course.'

'Well, I think it's horrible,' said Sophia.

'The man isn't an ordinary sort of criminal. He's young and handsome and comes from a good family,' Gerald explained. 'He killed a rich and famous prostitute. They had been seeing each other for a long time, and it seems that she had always been afraid he would kill her for her jewels.'

'Then why did she see him?' asked Sophia.

35 'Because she liked being afraid. Some women only enjoy themselves when they are terrified. Strange, isn't it?'

Just then a tall, middle-aged woman came in wearing a dress that no one could fail to notice. It blazed with red and gold and black. She was followed by a young Englishman in evening dress with beautifully arranged whiskers. They sat down at the table next to the one Sophia and Gerald were at. The woman looked round with large, scornful eyes at all the other people in the restaurant.

'That's one!' Gerald whispered to Sophia.

'One what?' Sophia whispered back.

Gerald raised his eyebrows to warn her and closed one eye. 'Prostitute,' he said very softly.

He had not spoken quite softly enough, however. The Englishman had heard, and a look of cold displeasure passed across his proud face.

It was obvious that he belonged to a class much higher than Gerald's, and that Gerald knew it. Gerald was wealthy, but he did not come from a rich old family. He did not have the habit of wealth. Much of Gerald's money had been gained by hard work, but this Englishman with the whiskers had never worked for a penny in his life. He had the face of someone who was used to giving orders. He knew he could have anything he wanted. He was absolutely sure of himself. That his companion did not listen to him much or even look at him seemed not to bother him at all. When she spoke, it was in French. He would reply briefly in English.

## Wonderful manners

Gerald talked to Sophia more loudly. With that upper-class Englishman listening, he could not feel anything but uneasy. He began to talk about money and travel. However, although he was trying to impress the Englishman, he was only making himself look ridiculous.

The Englishman was having a little trouble understanding his companion's French.

'Excuse me,' Gerald said to him. 'Madame is talking about the execution the day after tomorrow.'

The Englishman looked at Gerald angrily, but the woman smiled at him, and from then on insisted on talking to her friend through him.

Just then a slim young Frenchman with a pale face came into the restaurant. When he saw Gerald, he gave a surprised smile. He came across and shook hands with him warmly.

'This is my wife,' said Gerald, introducing Sophia, taking
5  care to pronounce his words clearly like a man who knows he has had just a little too much to drink.

The young man kissed Sophia's hand, and Gerald introduced him as Monsieur Chirac, a friend of his from the time when he had lived in Paris before.

10  The two men talked together in French. Sophia understood little, but she could see that Gerald was surprised and impressed by what Chirac told him. Then Chirac went off to another table.

Sophia was beginning to be afraid that Gerald was
15  behaving differently from usual. She did not think he was drunk. Such an idea would have shocked her. However, she was not too sure that she was thinking very clearly herself. She decided it might be better if they left.

'Gerald,' she said in a low voice. 'I'm feeling tired.'
20  'You don't want to go, do you?' he asked, looking hurt.

The lady at the next table began to talk to him again, and he ordered something else to drink. When he mentioned seeing Hortense, she was impressed. Her friend frowned irritably at them, and then said, 'Are you talking about
25  Hortense Schneider?'

'Yes,' said Gerald. 'My wife and I met her this afternoon.'

'She's in Trouville,' said the man bluntly.

Gerald shook his head.

'I had supper with her in Trouville last night,' said the
30  Englishman. 'And she's acting at the theatre there tonight.'

'If what you say is true, then it seems odd that we saw her in Paris this afternoon, doesn't it?' said Gerald.

'If you want to insult me, sir—' the man said icily.

'Gerald!' Sophia urged him in a whisper.
35  'Be quiet!' Gerald replied angrily.

Then suddenly the Englishman nodded towards the door and said, 'Hadn't we better settle this outside?' He sounded quite drunk too.

'I am at your service!' said Gerald, rising.

The Englishman went out of the restaurant without a word to his companion. Gerald said to Sophia, who was overcome with terror, 'Wait here. I shall be back in a minute.' Then he went out too.

Monsieur Chirac was still sitting at a table with two other men and three women. The Englishman's companion got up and joined them.

Sophia waited alone feeling helpless and ashamed. There was nothing she could do. Almost an hour later, at twenty minutes past three, Monsieur Chirac came over to her. He bowed, and said, 'Madame, will you allow me to take you to your hotel?'

'But the bill?' she stammered. 'It isn't paid, and I have no money.'

'I'll see to that,' he answered.

They got into a taxi, and Monsieur Chirac left her at the door of her hotel. Sophia thought she had never before met a man with such wonderful manners.

She went up to the room, coldly angry with her husband. Gerald was a fool. That he should have allowed himself to get drunk was bad enough, but that he should have left her in the horrible situation from which Monsieur Chirac had rescued her was disgraceful. He had behaved stupidly.

At dawn, there was a sound outside the door. Gerald came in, smelling strongly of drink and with his lip bleeding. Sophia noticed that he was no longer drunk.

'Monsieur Chirac brought me home,' she said.

'I asked you to wait for me,' Gerald said sharply. He was trying to hide from himself the fact that he had behaved like a fool.

'I don't think you need talk like that,' Sophia answered. She felt that he was being unjust, but she was wise enough to stop at that and just accept it.

'I knocked my chin against the side of the steps as I was coming up,' Gerald said.

She knew that that was a lie, but answered kindly, 'Did you? Let me wash it.'

# 8
# Fever

## Auxerre

Sophia went to sleep feeling miserable, but when she woke up a few hours later in the expensive room that Gerald had taken for them, she was in a much happier mood. She
5 was too proud to admit that she had married a charming fool, so she decided that Gerald had been right and she had been wrong. She had left the restaurant with another man when Gerald had told her to wait. If she had been Gerald, she would have been much angrier than he had been.

10 Sophia and Gerald had an early lunch together.

'I was planning to go to Auxerre this afternoon,' Gerald said. 'Chirac has to go there for his newspaper, so I thought I'd go too.'

Suddenly, Sophia remembered that that was where the
15 execution of the murderer Rivain was to be.

'Not to see the execution?' she stammered.

'Why not? I've always wanted to see one. You can do exactly as you like. Either stay here or come with me. You don't have to watch the execution if you go.'

20 'Of course I'll go,' she said quietly.

Sophia had always been used to never doing anything without making careful plans first, but in Gerald's world, it was the opposite. They were having their coffee at the end of their meal when Chirac suddenly arrived, reminded them of
25 the train times and then hurried off, either to his office or to his home. In less than a quarter of an hour, Gerald was pushing into his pocket a fat brown envelope which had come in the post that morning, and they were in a taxi driving rapidly to the railway station. They caught the train
30 with less than a minute to spare.

When they arrived at Auxerre, they found that the execution had affected local prices. No taxi driver would take them to the hotel for less than ten francs. The usual price was two. In the end, they decided to walk to the hotel, with Gerald carrying their heavy luggage.

The hotel had one small room to offer, at the price of twenty-five francs.

'How terrible that ordinary travellers can't get a proper room at a proper price just because there's going to be an execution tomorrow!' complained Gerald. 'We will try somewhere else.'

A taxi driver said he knew of another hotel, and offered to take them there for five francs. When they arrived, Gerald went in. After a few minutes, he appeared at an upstairs window and shouted down, 'It's all right.'

'How much do they want?' Sophia asked.

Gerald hesitated. 'Thirty-five francs,' he said. 'We're lucky to get it even at that.'

Gerald came down and gave the taxi driver the five francs. The man then demanded a tip. Gerald had nothing less than a two-franc coin, so he gave him that.

There was no porter at the hotel. Gerald had to carry the luggage upstairs himself. When Sophia saw the small bed in the dirty room, she remarked, 'We can't both sleep in this bed; it's not large enough for two.'

'Oh, I shan't go to bed,' Gerald said. 'It's for you.'

## The guillotine

After they had eaten in the dirty hotel dining room, Sophia went to bed; but noises from inside and outside the hotel prevented her from sleeping. Again she felt deeply unhappy. The faces of the other people in the dining room had seemed to her to be cruel and shameless. She thought it rather frightening that so many people should want to see an execution. She had been shocked, too, to learn that the execution was to take place in the square outside the hotel.

At daybreak, Sophia went to the window and looked out. There were people walking about in the square. Among them she saw Gerald and Chirac. They were talking to two girls.

A group of workmen arrived and began to set up the guillotine. The crowd grew, and the noise became more threatening. When the machine was ready, the executioner tried the blade. Twice he let it fall, and both times the shouts
5 from the crowds became deafening. Women sitting at the windows of the houses round the square screamed and clapped happily. The excitement of the people made it seem like a festival.

Sophia was tired. She slept a little, but was awoken again
10 by a great noise of screaming and shouting. She went to the window. The first thing she saw was Gerald coming out of a house opposite, followed by the girl she had seen him talking to earlier.

Then, from a little street behind the guillotine, a priest appeared, followed by the handsome man who was going to have his head cut off.

'Why do I stay here and watch?' Sophia asked herself hysterically. But she did not move. All she could do was look at the gleaming triangle of metal, hanging high above the head of the man lying below it, waiting.

Only a short time previously, Sophia had been an
25 innocent, timid creature in Bursley, just a foolish girl who thought that keeping letters secret was the greatest excitement. Now she was watching this terrifying sight. Either that day or this, it seemed to her, was not real.

Suddenly, the metal flashed in the sunlight. There was
30 the sound of the guillotine blade falling. Sophia sank down

on the floor in terror and hid her face, trembling, while a mad shout came from the crowd in the square.

Minutes later, there was a knock at the door and Sophia opened it. Chirac was standing outside, holding on to Gerald by his arm. Chirac was clearly exhausted, but Gerald was worse. He looked like a dead man. His curiosity, it seemed, had been stronger than his stomach. He staggered past her into the room and fell onto the bed.

A woman now came into the room. She was the owner of the hotel. She began to talk to Sophia in French.

'She wants sixty francs,' Chirac translated. Chirac explained that Gerald had agreed to pay a hundred francs for the room; fifty in advance and another fifty after the execution. The other ten was for the dinner. Sophia was shocked, but she did not mention Gerald's lie to her about the price of the room. In fact, Chirac knew about it.

'Gerald! Do you hear?' she said coldly.

Gerald only groaned, so she took his wallet out of his pocket and paid the woman. Then Chirac left to go back to Paris with the report for his newspaper, and Gerald went to sleep.

So this was what he had brought her to! The horrors of the night, the dawn and the morning! What a fool he was.

Sticking out of the pocket of his dirty coat was the brown envelope he had received the day before. She took it out and looked inside. She found 200 pounds in English banknotes in it. She quietly took the money and tore up the envelope, hiding the pieces on the top shelf of a high cupboard. Then, while Gerald slept, she quietly sewed the banknotes into the lining of her skirt.

That she was stealing did not worry her a great deal. She had an idea that with a man like Gerald she might find herself one day in the most impossible of situations. Having the money allowed her to be less dependent on him. When he discovered his loss, she would say she knew nothing about a brown envelope. Actually, when he woke up, he thought that it must have been taken from his pocket when he was in the square.

# A moment of triumph

For a time, both Gerald and Sophia thought that 12,000 pounds was an enormous amount of money that would last forever. Gerald planned not to spend more than 600 a year, which is less than two pounds a day. Actually he never spent less than that each day just on hotel bills. After a year or two, he and Sophia moved to a cheaper hotel. Then, one day he said to Sophia, 'I am completely out of money. I haven't got even five francs left.'

'Well, what do you expect me to do?' Sophia asked. She was now twenty-four years old, and even more beautiful than when Gerald had married her. She had also become charming and arrogant during her time in Paris.

'Why don't you write home to your family and ask them for money?' he suggested.

'Ask my family for money?' she repeated sarcastically. Did he seriously imagine that she was willing to beg from her family?

'We shall starve if you don't.'

'All right, we shall starve,' said Sophia.

Gerald hurried out of the room.

Sophia suspected that Gerald might be lying about having no money. She decided to do something she had never done before—spy on him. Quickly she put on her hat and gloves, and hurried out of the hotel.

Gerald had not got far. He was walking cheerfully along the other side of the street, looking at every woman under forty. She saw him stop and buy a cigar. He tore away the paper around it, and threw the paper to the ground. He lit the cigar and walked on. Sophia, not far behind, picked up the piece of paper.

Gerald came back at about nine o'clock. He looked as if he had been drinking. Sophia was already in bed.

'I'm quite without any money,' he said as he staggered across the room. 'I'm sure your family would be glad to lend us some till I get some more. I'd pay for you to go back to Bursley if I had any money, but I haven't.'

'Liar!' she said.

'Oh, so I am a liar now, am I?' he said. He added, more to himself than to her, 'Well, this has got to end, this has!' He took down his trunk from the top of the cupboard, and began to pack his clothes.

When he had finished, and was pushing the trunk out of the room, she said, 'Here! You're forgetting this.' She held up a thin circle of red paper.

'What's that?' asked Gerald.

'It is from the cigar you bought this afternoon.'

He hesitated, then swore violently and hurried out of the room. After all he had made her suffer, Sophia enjoyed her moment of triumph. She never forgot it.

Sophia passed a night of misery, but early the following morning there was an unexpected knock at the door. The waiter had brought a card. It was Chirac's.

'The gentleman wanted your husband,' the waiter said, 'but when I told him he had gone, he asked for you.'

The waiter went. He returned with Chirac.

When Chirac saw her, he was worried. 'You look ill,' he said.

'I have a dreadful headache. Do you want Gerald? He has left me.'

'It's not possible!' he breathed. 'Ah, the miserable man! Do you know where he has gone?'

'No. What do you want?' asked Sophia.

'Yesterday afternoon he borrowed some money from me.'

Now Sophia knew why Gerald had gone out.

'He said that 5,000 francs should have arrived for him yesterday morning, but it was late, and he needed 500 until this morning. I did not have that amount, so I borrowed it from the office cash box. It is absolutely necessary for me to put it back this morning.' Then he added, 'You did not know that he was coming to borrow money from me?'

'No,' replied Sophia. This seemed to her to be the worst proof of Gerald's dishonesty. 'Luckily, I have enough to repay you,' she said. 'Please wait for me downstairs.'

After he had gone, she removed some of the English banknotes from the lining of her skirt and took them down to Chirac. They went to a bank together to change them so he could have his 500 francs.

In the taxi taking them back to the hotel, Chirac said, 'How can I thank you? Truly—' Suddenly, he felt a heavy
5  weight against his shoulder. Sophia had fainted, and slipped down against him, unconscious.

## Madame Foucault

When she opened her eyes, Sophia found herself not with Chirac in the taxi, but lying in bed in a dark but well-furnished
10  room. A man she had never seen before was standing at the side of the bed. He was looking at her, and appeared to be telling her to do things. She could not hear what he was saying. He must be a doctor, she thought, but she did not want to reply or move.

15  For some time, she did little but lie in bed and sleep. Then, slowly, she began to recover.

One day she discovered where she was, and what had happened to her. She had fainted in the taxi opposite the house of a Madame Foucault, a rather fat middle-aged lady. Madame
20  Foucault had just come out of her house, and thinking the taxi had stopped for her, had got in. When she found Chirac and Sophia inside, and saw that Sophia was ill, she had insisted that Chirac should carry Sophia into her house. Then she called for the doctor, and it was discovered that Sophia was
25  very ill. Madame Foucault had said she should stay in the house instead of going to a hospital because everyone knew that the Paris hospitals were terrible. Since then Madame Foucault and another woman, Madame Laurence, who lived in the house, had looked after Sophia. Six weeks passed before
30  Sophia was well enough to understand all this.

'How kind you have both been!' Sophia said to Madame Foucault and Madame Laurence when she realized how much had been done for her.

Madame Foucault told her that she must not talk, and that
35  Chirac would be coming back soon. He had been away, she said, and added that he was 'a charming boy'.

One day, when Sophia had almost fully recovered from her illness, Madame Foucault came to tell her that she had to go out for a while. She said that Madame Laurence might be going out, too.

Some hours later, Sophia heard a carriage stop in front of the house. She went to the window, and saw Madame Foucault and a young man get out of it—the young man was Madame Foucault's boyfriend.

That evening, there were sounds of a violent argument in Madame Foucault's room. Sophia could hear Madame Foucault sobbing noisily. The door of the room opened suddenly, a man's angry voice said, 'I've had enough. Let go of me, please!' There was the sound of a struggle, and then Sophia heard the man go downstairs and leave.

Sophia got up and went to Madame Foucault's room. She found the woman lying there on the floor, sobbing hysterically. There was nothing really wrong with her. Her anger and self-pity were just too much for her. As Sophia bent down, feelings of sympathy were mixed with disgust at the sight of that fat body and the wrinkled, painted face.

'Keep calm, please, Madame Foucault!' Sophia said. She tried to speak soothingly, but she found it difficult. Her reason told her that she should feel sympathy for this aging, hysterical woman, who had done so much for her, but her heart was unwilling.

Madame Laurence walked in. She had been out to a restaurant. 'What is the matter?' she asked.

'He has left me!' Madame Foucault sobbed. 'He is the last. I have no one now!'

'He'll be back!' Madame Laurence said, and she and Sophia together helped Madame Foucault get up off the floor. They persuaded her to lie on her bed.

'Oh, why has he gone! I have never treated a man badly in my life,' sobbed Madame Foucault.

Madame Laurence went off to her room.

'It wasn't always like this, you know,' Madame Foucault continued, speaking to Sophia. 'I once owned a hotel. I was wealthy. Ten years ago I was spending 100,000 francs a year.

But I knew things could not go on that way forever. That is why I moved in here. I borrowed money to pay for the furniture, and then I let three bedrooms. By serving meals too, I make sufficient to live on.'

5 'Then that', Sophia interrupted, pointing to her own bedroom, 'is your room?'

'Yes. I put you in it because all the others were let. Now I have nothing, and I owe so much. And he chooses this moment to leave me! He is twenty-five, and I love him.'

10 'You must not forget that I owe you quite a lot of money,' said Sophia, trying to ignore the details of Madame Foucault's love affairs.

Madame Foucault said that she would not like to accept money from her, but Sophia knew that this was just a 15 pretence.

'How long have I been here?' asked Sophia.

'I don't know. Eight weeks—or is it nine?'

'Let's say nine. How much must I pay a week?' asked Sophia.

20 'I don't want anything! You are a friend of Chirac's—'

'No, naturally I must pay,' Sophia interrupted. 'Shall I pay you seventy-five francs a week?'

'That is too much!' Madame Foucault objected, without really meaning it.

25 'What? For all you have done for me?' Sophia was happy to pay it. She counted out the money.

After a moment, Madame Foucault burst into tears. 'You are so beautiful,' she sobbed. 'I am so glad that I made them bring you here.'

30 Suddenly, Sophia felt moved. 'Never can I forget how kind you and Madame Laurence have been to me,' she said softly.

At that moment, Madame Laurence returned to see how Madame Foucault was. 'You are looking tired,' she whispered to Sophia. 'You are too pale. All this emotion is 35 not good for you.' She pushed Sophia gently towards her room.

Sophia suddenly noticed how exhausted she felt, and gladly returned to her bed.

# 9
# Success

## A victory

Madame Laurence walked into Sophia's room one morning with a serious look on her face. 'War has been declared,' she said.

'No. What war?' asked Sophia. 5

'War with Germany. The city is quite excited. They say our armies will be in Berlin in a month—or at most two,' Madame Laurence replied.

'Why is there a war?' asked Sophia.

'Nobody knows.' 10

About a fortnight later, Chirac came. The sight of his extreme pleasure on seeing her was the sweetest thing that had happened to Sophia for years.

'Then you are cured?' he said, looking at her carefully.

'Quite.' 15

He sighed and said, 'It is an immense relief to me to know that. You gave me a terrible fright, my dear madame!' Then he added in a low voice, 'I owe you my most sincere apologies for bringing you to this place.'

'But why? Madame Foucault and Madame Laurence have 20 been most kind,' Sophia said.

'I suppose you are going back to England now?'

She shook her head.

'Then what will you do, if I may ask?'

'I don't know,' she answered honestly. She could not bear 25 the thought of facing her family and having them receive her back with forgiveness—she would prefer almost anything to that.

'You have heard nothing of him?' asked Chirac.

'Of whom? Gerald? Nothing!' 30

'Listen,' he suggested shyly, 'will you come for a drive with me?'

'With pleasure,' she agreed warmly.

The fresh air and bright sunshine and the joyful sense of freedom in being out in the streets made Sophia feel almost drunk.

5 'Do I still look ill?' she asked Chirac suddenly.

Chirac hesitated. 'Yes!' he said at last. 'But it suits you. You are more beautiful than ever.'

She smiled, and gave herself up happily to his admiration. Monsieur Chirac had the most wonderful 10 manners.

As the taxi went on, they noticed a crowd shouting and cheering. The driver turned and said, 'There has been a victory!'

'A victory!' murmured Chirac. 'Can it be possible?'

15 They stopped in a crowded square; the people there were very excited. A woman climbed up onto the taxi beside the driver, and began to sing the 'Marseillaise'—the famous song of the French Revolution. As she sang, the tears ran down her cheeks. The crowd joined in. Soon many were weeping, or 20 looking serious and brave, as if, should the moment ever come for them to die for their country, nothing could stop them. Feelings ran strong and deep. Sophia was caught up in it too and began to sob. Chirac leant out of the taxi and shook hands with a man who was standing beside it.

25 'Who is that?' Sophia asked.

'I don't know,' said Chirac. He, too, was weeping like a child. 'Victory! Victory! How wonderful!'

## The furniture

When Sophia got back to her room, two badly dressed 30 middle-aged men were standing outside the door. One of them was the concierge—the watchman. When she opened the door and went in, the men pushed in after her.

'What do you want?' she said irritably.

'This man is from the authorities,' explained the 35 concierge. 'I regret it, but ...'

'Is it about the rent?' asked Sophia.

'No, the furniture,' the man replied.

Then Sophia learnt the truth about the furniture. The concierge said he had sold the furniture to Madame Foucault, but she had not paid for it. He had warned her again and again that she must pay. He had been very patient, he said, *5* and allowed her plenty of time. Now that time was finished. She must pay, or the furniture would be taken back.

Madame Foucault had gone out that morning; she knew she could not pay, and it seemed she did not want to see her furniture being removed. *10*

'Well,' said Sophia, 'I suppose you will allow me to pack up my own things?'

'Of course, madame!' the concierge replied.

As she was packing, she heard the sound of people arguing at the front door. Soon Madame Foucault burst into *15* the room.

'Save me! Save me, Madame Scales!' she begged. 'I did what I could for you!'

Sophia hated her for her loss of dignity, but what she said was true. *20*

'But what can I do?' she asked unwillingly.

'Lend me the money.'

'How much is it?'

'Less than 1,000 francs!' Madame Foucault knelt down on the floor in front of Sophia, which disgusted her. *25*

'Please get up,' said Sophia, not sure what to do.

'I shall repay you, I promise,' Madame Foucault claimed. 'I swear it!'

'No,' Sophia said to Madame Foucault, 'I won't lend you the money. But I'll buy the furniture. And I'll promise to sell *30* it to you as soon as you can pay me.'

'You are an angel of charity!' cried Madame Foucault, putting her arms round Sophia and hugging her tightly. 'Ah, you English women! You are so astonishing.'

Sophia was not an angel of charity. What she had *35* promised to do would result in a certain amount of trouble and worry to herself without the hope of any reward, but it was not charity. The sale was arranged.

The next morning, Sophia saw in the newspaper that the news of the victory which had sent the city mad had been entirely false. Tears came into her eyes. Her heart bled for France and for Chirac.

5
## The sweetest boy

There was a kind of plan that Madame Foucault and Sophia should work together to let rooms, so one afternoon, when Madame Foucault came into Sophia's room with a rather guilty expression on her face, Sophia half knew what she was
10    going to say. 'A lady and a gentleman are here,' Madame Foucault said. 'They want a bedroom.'

'Are they married?' asked Sophia.

'Ah! You know, one cannot ask to see people's marriage papers.'

15    'Has the lady been here before?'

'Yes,' replied Madame Foucault.

'With the same man?'

'No.'

'So why do you ask? You know what my reply will be,'
20    said Sophia.

'You will leave me if I allow them in?' asked Madame Foucault, looking worried.

'Yes,' said Sophia curtly.

'And you will take your furniture with you …!'
25    Sophia said nothing.

'But how am I to live?' Madame Foucault asked feebly.

'By being respectable, and by only letting your rooms to respectable people!'

'Oh, I do not like this. But you are so much stronger than I
30    am,' murmured the elder woman. She gave a little sob, and went away.

That evening, Sophia knew that Madame Foucault was still upset. She heard her crying in her room, and she saw that nothing was being done about the evening meal. With
35    kindness in her heart, but not on her tongue, Sophia went to her and said, 'Shall I cook dinner this evening?'

'That would be most kind of you,' said Madame Foucault, and she sobbed even more loudly.

Sophia went to the grocer's. Not only did she buy food for dinner, but she also discovered the grocer was looking for somewhere to live. Sophia arranged for him to rent one of the rooms in the house. Madame Foucault was deeply impressed by Sophia's actions. She had never taken in such a respectable boarder before.

The next day, they both worked hard cleaning and tidying the rooms. At four o'clock, Madame Foucault suggested going out for a walk. Sophia agreed.

The streets of Paris that evening were as bright and colourful as ever. All the cafés and restaurants seemed to be full of laughing, cheerful people. Nobody would have guessed that France had just been heavily defeated by the Germans. The Empire of Napoleon III was finished, and France was once again a republic.

Suddenly, Sophia noticed that Madame Foucault was no longer beside her. She looked round, and saw her talking to the young man who had left her so angrily. She watched them for a while, and then went home alone.

Two days went by and Madame Foucault did not return home. Then a letter arrived. In it, Madame Foucault informed Sophia that her lover had said Paris would soon be dangerous. He had insisted that she should go with him to Brussels. Madame Foucault wrote:

*He is the sweetest boy. He adores me, and I am so happy. He would not let me come and tell you about it: he said we had to go immediately. We love each other so much. He has spent almost 2,000 francs on clothes for me ...*

And so on. No word of apology.

'Young fool! Fool!' Sophia burst out angrily. She did not mean herself. She meant the young man who seemed to love that fat, ugly, horrible woman so deeply. That was the last Sophia ever heard of Madame Foucault.

## Monsieur Niepce

Many people were escaping from the danger that they felt coming ever closer to Paris. Sophia still had about a hundred pounds; she could have left quite easily if she had wanted to. But she was too busy looking after her boarder, Monsieur Niepce—the grocer.

Chirac visited Sophia every day at this time. 'The Germans will come to Paris,' he said in despair. He, too, rented a room in the house, and then introduced another newspaper man who wanted a room. So Sophia now had all the rooms full, and a good rent coming in.

The siege of Paris by the Germans began. Soon people were short of food. The price of everything went up. Sophia increased the rents of her rooms as well as the price of her meals. Then a friend of Monsieur Niepce came looking for a room, and Sophia gave him hers. She used the little servant's room at the top of the house as her own bedroom.

Sophia was a great success with her boarders. She was a good businesswoman, clean, tidy and strict, and she was an excellent cook. She managed the house and the meals so well that they regarded her as quite miraculous. They were all married men except Chirac; their wives had been sent away from Paris to places of safety.

Sophia had one servant, but one morning she did not appear, so Sophia took the breakfasts to the rooms herself. When she was in Monsieur Niepce's room, the old man suddenly put his arm round her waist.

Sophia stood perfectly still.

'It is true that I have a wife,' he began to say to her, 'but she is far away. I love you madly. I know I am old, but I am rich.' Then he went on in a respectful voice. 'If you will be kind to me, Madame Scales, I will give you 2,000 francs a month and anything you want from my shop.'

Sophia felt like telling him to get out of her house at once. But then she reminded herself that he was a good boarder. He always paid his rent on time. Today, he was just behaving foolishly.

'If you want to stay with me, Monsieur Niepce,' she said with cruel calmness, 'you must be respectable. Do not be stupid. Do not be such an old fool!'

Monsieur Niepce went back to his shop. Sophia hoped that none of the other boarders had heard what Monsieur Niepce had said. She thought Chirac might have been in his room, writing.

That night, Sophia woke up suddenly. She wondered what time it was. She looked at her watch, but it had stopped; she had forgotten to wind it up. She had to get up in time to start work at six o'clock, so she lit a candle and went down to the kitchen to look at the clock.

Suddenly, Chirac appeared in the corridor. 'So you have decided to sell yourself to him!' he whispered. He looked angry and disgusted.

'What time is it?' Sophia asked.

'Three o'clock,' Chirac sneered.

'I forgot to wind my watch,' Sophia explained.

'Really?' Chirac sneered again.

'Not so loud,' Sophia said. 'You will wake the others!'

'And Monsieur Niepce—will he need to be woken up?' asked Chirac sarcastically.

'Monsieur Niepce is not here,' she said calmly. She pushed Monsieur Niepce's door open. The room was empty and showed no signs of anyone having slept in it.

Chirac's face fell.

Sophia took her watch out and said, 'And now wind up my watch for me, and set it, please.'

She saw that he was terribly embarrassed. Tears came into his eyes. Then he ran into his room and banged the door shut.

She too cried when she got back to her room, and went on doing so for a long time. 'What a shame! What a shame!' she said.

## Friendship

Their relations were permanently changed. For several days, Sophia and Chirac did not meet at all. When, at the end of the week, Chirac had to face Sophia to pay his bill, it was clear that he thought of himself as a criminal who had no defence for his crime.

A few days after that, Monsieur Niepce tried to bring a charming young woman into his room, and Sophia accidentally caught them in the corridor. She was angry, but showed it only in her cold steel-like voice. She had become a tough woman—without knowing it!

The next day, Chirac knocked at the kitchen door and said, 'I must give notice that I shall have to leave.'

'Why?' she asked bluntly.

'My newspaper has been closed down, and I can't pay the rent any more.'

'You can pay me later when you get some money.'

He shook his head. 'I cannot accept your kindness.'

'Haven't you got any money at all?'

'None.'

'Then you will have to get into debt somewhere.'

'Yes, but not here! Not to you!' said Chirac.

'Truly, Chirac, you are not being reasonable.'

'But that's how it is.'

'That's not how it is going to be!' Sophia said in a firm voice. 'I insist that you stay, and you will repay me when you can.'

'You are too good. But it hurts me to accept—'

'Oh, your stupid pride! Is that what you call friendship? Go away now. How can I get on with the cooking while you stand there arguing with me!'

But in three days, Chirac was lucky enough to get a job on another paper.

## Chirac loves Sophia

On Christmas morning, Chirac came to Sophia in the kitchen again. He invited her to go out for lunch with him.

'What an idea!' she said. 'How can I leave? I have to get lunch ready.'

But he insisted, and at a quarter past twelve they went out into the sad, empty streets. They arrived at a small café. Chirac was well known there, so he and Sophia were served excellent food.

During the meal, Chirac put his hand on Sophia's, and accidentally she looked into his eyes at the same moment. They both became self-conscious. She had not pulled her hand away at once, and so she could not do so at all after that.

'My dear, dear friend,' Chirac said as he put his arm round her waist, 'I love you.'

Her face hardened. 'You must not do that,' she said coldly, unkindly. Yet she did not want to stop him.

Respectfully and obediently he took his arm away. 'My very dear friend,' he urged, 'you must know that I love you.'

She shook her head impatiently. She knew that she was treating him badly, but she could not help herself. Then she began to feel sorry for him. She did not love him. But she was moved and flattered, and she wanted to love him.

'Let me hope,' said Chirac.

'My poor Chirac!' she murmured.

He seized her again by the waist. She drew her face away. She was neither hard nor angry. Not knowing how to understand her pity, he let go of her.

'My poor Chirac,' she said again, 'I ought not to have come. It is perfectly useless.'

'No, no!' he whispered fiercely.

They left the restaurant silently. Sophia quietly thought about the hopeless problem of existence, for it seemed to her that she and Chirac had almost created this sadness out of
5 nothing. And yet it was a sadness so deep, so incurable.

## Chirac's decision

Sophia lay awake one night thinking about Chirac. His behaviour since Christmas had frightened her. He had lost his appetite, and eaten almost nothing. He went about with
10 the face of a man dying of a broken heart. 'Have I done this to him?' Sophia asked herself.

It seemed to her strange that she had first encouraged and then repulsed him. All the time she knew that she longed for love. But she wanted a different kind of love—something
15 calm, regular, rather serious. In the end, she decided that she had been right to refuse him.

Suddenly, there was a smell of burning in the house. She went out into the corridor. The smell came from Chirac's room. She went in without knocking.

20 She had left a saucepan of soup on a small cooking lamp beside his bed that evening. All that he had to do when he came home was light the lamp and put the saucepan on it. In fact he had lit the lamp, turned it full on, but then fallen asleep in his chair. Smoke was coming from the lamp. Sophia
25 hurried forwards and turned the lamp down.

She looked at Chirac. He was a sad sight. He looked like a dead person. Without thinking, she put the saucepan of soup on top of the lamp. The noise woke him up.

'You nearly burnt the house down,' Sophia said to him.

30 He jumped up as if in a dream, but Sophia made him sit down again.

'I wanted to tell you', he said, 'that I am going away, out of Paris, by balloon—for my newspaper … it is an important job, and I offered myself.'

35 'Won't it be dangerous?' she said.

'Yes, it will,' he answered. 'But what will you …?'

She wished she had not
mentioned danger. It hurt her to
watch him struggling with his emotions so.

'It will be the night after tomorrow,' he said, 'at the Gare
du Nord. I do hope you will come and wish me goodbye.' 5

'Of course, if you really want me to,' she replied.

Two nights later, Sophia found Chirac in the courtyard of
the Gare du Nord railway station. He was talking to the men
who were getting the balloon ready. She waited for him to
finish, and then walked over to him. 10

'I hope you will have a safe journey,' she said.

'I am so pleased you have come, madame. It is because of
you that I am leaving Paris,' said Chirac.

She frowned.

'Ah!' he begged in a whisper. 'Don't do that, Sophia. 15
Smile at me. After all, it is not my fault. Remember that this
may be the last time I see you.'

Chirac got into the balloon with another man, who was to
try to guide it in the right direction. The ropes that held the
balloon were untied, and it rose quickly into the dark night. 20

Of the sixty-five balloons that left Paris during the siege,
two were lost. This was the first of the two. Nobody ever saw
Chirac or the other man again. It was thought that the sea
must have swallowed them.

# 10
# Reunited

## The new guest

By 1871 the siege of Paris was over. Sophia continued to make a living and to save money. Then one day she saw an advertisement saying that a pension—a small hotel—was for sale. She bought it. It was called the Pension Frensham.

As the new owner and manager, Sophia turned the Pension Frensham into an excellent small hotel, where the prices were modest, and where the guests had to be respectable. By the end of 1878, the 200 pounds she had taken from Gerald Scales had become 2,000. She never heard a word from her husband or from her own family.

One day a new guest arrived at the Pension Frensham. He was clearly of a different class to all the others. He was a young man of about twenty-five. He was not handsome, but he was elegant in his clothes and in his manners. Some of the other guests thought he might be a young lord, but really he came from a family of pottery manufacturers.

The young man's name was Matthew Peel-Swynnerton, and he had only about fifty francs in his pocket because he had been making a fool of himself with women in the more expensive parts of Paris. He had come to the Pension Frensham for the last few days of his holiday because there he could be absolutely sure of spending not more than twelve francs a day.

On his first night at the pension, he decided to stay in and have an early night. As he crossed the hall, he saw the owner sitting in her small office. 'Excuse me, Mrs Scales,' he said politely. 'Have any letters come for me tonight?' He knew that this was impossible since nobody knew his address.

'What name?' Sophia asked with cold politeness.

'Peel-Swynnerton,' he answered. He watched her. If this Mrs Scales was the long-lost aunt of his friend Cyril Povey, she must know those two names, which were so famous in Bursley. Did she look surprised? At first he thought so, but after a moment he was sure that she had noticed nothing. Then she turned towards the place where the letters were kept. He saw, for the first time, her face from the side. She looked exactly like Cyril. There could be no mistake.

'No,' she said quietly. 'I see no letters here for you.'

'Have you had anyone called Povey staying here recently?' Matthew asked nervously. 'Cyril Povey, of Bursley?'

Her voice seemed to tremble a little when she replied, 'Not that I remember. Were you expecting him to be here?'

'Well, it wasn't a definite arrangement,' he mumbled. 'Thank you. Goodnight.'

'Goodnight,' she said.

'What a surprising thing!' the young man thought as he walked up the stairs. He had discovered the woman who had run away from Bursley before he was born, and of whom nobody knew anything. What news for Cyril!

## A blaze of love

That night, Sophia felt sad as she got into bed. Her head was full of questions. Had Constance married Mr Povey, she wondered, and did she have a grown-up son? And was her own mother dead? Sophia knew that her boarders and guests thought she was a wise woman. But she had been foolish to cut herself off from her family so completely. She was getting old, and she was alone in the world. There was nothing to stop her going back to Bursley and putting things right. Nothing except the fact that her whole soul refused to go!

Did Peel-Swynnerton suspect who she was? 'No!' she said to herself finally. 'The whole idea is just too silly. Anyway, I've lived alone for so long, and I'll stay as I am.'

It seemed as if a decision had been made, but in fact these thoughts about her family greatly disturbed Sophia. By daybreak, she had a fever. She was quite ill, and the doctor made her stay in bed for a few days.

Not long after this, Sophia received a letter from Constance. So her suspicions about Mr Peel-Swynnerton had been correct after all!

The letter said:

5   *My darling Sophia,*

*I cannot tell you how delighted I was to learn that after all these years you are alive and well, and so successful, too. I long to see you, my dear sister… Surely now you will come and visit me.*

10   *Mr Critchlow tells me to say that there is a lot of money waiting for you. He is the trustee of Mother's and Father's wills, and also Aunt Harriet's.*

*Fondest love, Constance*

15   The spirit of simple love in the letter suddenly woke a similar spirit in Sophia for Constance. She wrote back, filling her letter with a blaze of love; but she said she would not visit Bursley. If Constance chose to come and see her in Paris, that would make her happier than anything, but she herself

20   would not move.

Things after that were never the same at the Pension Frensham. Sophia's health would not allow her to work as hard as she had done. The pension started to become less successful.

25   Sophia tried to get Constance to come and visit her, but Constance said she was too ill. She had sciatica—a terribly painful nervous condition that made it difficult for her to walk. It was getting worse, she said. She had to lie down every day after dinner to rest.

30   Sophia began to ask herself about her duty to Constance. The truth was that she was searching for an excuse to change her mind.

There was an Englishman in Paris who owned another pension. For some time he had been trying to buy the

35   Pension Frensham, but Sophia had always refused to sell. Now she wondered whether he was still interested.

One morning they met in the street, and once again he talked to her about his offer, 'Well, why don't you?' he urged her enthusiastically. 'Why not take a holiday for the rest of your life?'

She shook her head. 'I gave you my answer years ago,' she said in an obstinate way, while fearing that he might accept her words. 5

'Please think it over.'

They met again a few days later, and talked about the idea once more. 'There's only one thing that would make me change my mind,' Sophia remarked, 'and that is my sister's health.' For the sake of her pride, Sophia let him think that Constance was seriously ill, and thus, in time, she yielded. The Pension Frensham was sold. 10

## Sophia returns 15

The following spring, soon after dinner one day, Constance got ready to go to the railway station to meet Sophia. She had prepared the second bedroom for her with enormous care. She had also dressed with enormous care for their first meeting. She did not want to meet Sophia in one of her ordinary coats, but it would also, she thought, be a sad mistake to meet her in her best coat! 20

Constance was a little afraid of Sophia. In thirty years, Sophia might have grown into anything while Constance had remained just Constance. Yes, Constance was afraid, but she did not intend to show her fear in her best coat. She had dignity hidden under her mild outside; she decided on her second-best coat. 25

At the station she waited for the train. A lot of passengers got off, and then Constance saw a strange-looking dog in the crowd. Its head and shoulders were covered with thick hair, but the rest of its body had been shaved. It had a pink ribbon round its neck, which made it look even more outrageous. A chain ran from its collar. Holding on to the chain was a tall distinguished-looking woman dressed in beautiful clothes. It was Sophia! 30 35

The two sisters both hesitated, not quite recognizing each other. Then Sophia lied. 'I would have known you anywhere,' she remarked, smiling. They kissed.

5    'Did Cyril meet you in London?' asked Constance.

'Oh, yes!' said Sophia eagerly. 'And I went to his house. He's a delightful boy. I am very fond of him.'

She spoke exactly as Constance remembered. Her tone and the commanding movements of her hands sent
10 Constance's mind flying back to the 1860s. She could see that Sophia was used to giving orders and having people do as she told them.

When they got home, Sophia was polite to Amy, but in a cold, proud way, which Amy was not used to. Constance felt
15 quite nervous. Sophia had really become rather formidable, although Constance did not want to admit it.

At first, Constance tried to keep Sophia's dog, Fossette, away from her own little dog, Spot. Constance was afraid Fossette might attack Spot, but in fact the two dogs became
20 the best of friends.

When the two sisters had settled down, Constance asked Sophia gently, 'How long have you been a widow?'

Sophia blushed. 'I don't know that I am a widow. My husband left me in 1870, and I've never seen or heard of him
25 since.'

'Oh, my dear!' cried Constance. 'I thought you were a widow …' She stopped. She looked worried.

'Everyone always treated me as a widow in Paris,' said Sophia, 'and I may be a widow.'

'Of course,' said Constance quickly. 'I see …'

Then Mr and Mrs Critchlow came. Mr Critchlow wanted to discuss the money Sophia was to receive from her parents and her aunt. They went off together while Constance remained in the sitting room with Mrs Critchlow. Constance wondered to herself whether Sophia would have to tell Mr Critchlow that she was not sure that she was a widow. She thought that someone should try to find out whether anyone knew anything about Gerald Scales at Birkinshaws. But that might be dangerous. If Gerald was still alive, and as nasty as before, and caused Sophia trouble …!

Mr Critchlow asked Sophia what she thought of Cyril in a way that suggested that he, Mr Critchlow, did not like Cyril.

'I'm very fond of him,' Sophia answered sharply. 'I won't listen to a word said against him.'

At the back of her mind, Sophia wondered if Cyril had taken a special fancy to her, his clever aunt, while never bothering to charm his mother. In London, Cyril and Sophia had dazzled and conquered each other because in many ways they were alike. Constance was a plain person who could not dazzle anyone, and Sophia soon discovered that Cyril hardly ever came to see her.

When Constance and Sophia said goodnight that first night, there was a great amount of quiet controlled love, confidence and respect in both their voices. Then, just as Constance was getting into bed, there was a terrible noise from downstairs. The dogs seemed to be fighting. She opened her door and stepped out into the corridor.

'Constance,' a low voice called out.

Constance jumped. For a moment, she had forgotten she was not alone in that part of the house.

'Is that you, Constance?' Sophia whispered.

'Yes.'

'Well, don't bother to go down to the dogs. They'll stop soon. Fossette won't bite. I'm so sorry she's disturbing the house,' Sophia said.

The dogs did soon stop, but that short conversation in the dark affected Constance strangely.

## A rich woman

The next morning, Sophia got up early, went to the window and looked out. 'It would kill me if I had to live here,' she thought. 'How noisy, and dirty and horribly ugly it all is!' It
5  surprised her that Constance seemed not to notice any of this. Sophia decided that she would just be paying a visit, and then she would go back to France.

Paris had always seemed beautiful to Sophia, and she longed to be there, but the idea of leaving Constance worried
10  her. Sophia was a rich woman. She had bought the Pension Frensham cheap and sold it for great riches. Mr Critchlow had looked after her money well. He had built up for her about as much money as she had herself earned. She lacked nothing that money could buy. All she wanted now was to be
15  happy. She bitterly regretted that she had not had a child. In this she envied Constance. A child seemed to be the one thing worth having.

When Constance went down for breakfast that morning, she saw stretched across one side of the table an umbrella. It
20  was Sophia's present to her from Paris. It was the best umbrella it was possible to buy. The handle was of gold, set with a circle of precious stones, and there was gold on the tips of the ribs, too. It was this detail that surprised Constance, and delighted her. She adored it.

25  ## The slippers

The two sisters found they were very happy together. Their voices, when they spoke to one another privately, were often tender, and this secretly pleased them both. Sophia decided to stay longer than she had planned.

30  Sophia always wore soft slippers in the morning, so nobody could hear her as she walked about the house. These slippers were the direct cause of a crisis.

Sophia had been with Constance for about a month, when, one Sunday morning, she got up early and went to
35  Constance's bedroom. Constance's sciatica had seemed to be

getting worse, and she was rather worried about her. She found that Constance was still in terrible pain.

'You poor dear!' she said. 'I'll go down and make you some tea.'

'Oh, Amy will do it,' said Constance. 5

'No, I shall make it myself,' Sophia said firmly.

On her way down the stairs, Sophia heard Amy's voice coming from the kitchen. 'Oh, get out, you!' Amy was saying irritably, and then there was a yelp from Fossette. Sophia guessed that Amy was taking good care of Spot, but doing as 10 little as possible for Fossette. This worried her much more than Fossette's yelp. When she entered the kitchen, she said with icy politeness, 'Good morning, Amy.'

Amy looked up, surprised. 'Good morning, madam,' she muttered sullenly. She had been startled by Sophia's 15 suddenly appearing in the kitchen. She had not heard her coming.

Sophia saw Spot drinking milk out of a saucer while Fossette stood sadly under the table, watching. Amy knew that Sophia had heard her dog yelp, and Sophia knew that 20 she knew.

'Is that all the milk you give Fossette?' Sophia asked when it came to Fossette's turn. Fossette was bigger than Spot, but had only been given half as much.

'That's all there is left, madam,' said Amy sharply. 25

It was Sophia's soft slippers that had caused the crisis. Because of them Amy had not heard Sophia coming down the stairs.

Sophia made tea and took it up to Constance. When they had drunk it, Constance rang the bell for Amy. 'I'll ask her to 30 see if the postman has brought any letters,' she said. Sunday morning was the day when Constance usually received a letter from Cyril.

When Amy came up, Constance asked her about letters.

'There aren't any,' Amy answered, quite rudely. 'You know 35 that if there had been any, I would have brought them up. I wish you wouldn't call me upstairs for nothing. I'm always being interrupted, and it isn't as if I haven't got enough to do—especially now!' With the last two words she gave Sophia an angry stare.

'Amy!' said Sophia icily. 'Do not speak to your mistress like that—at least not while I am here. You know how ill and weak she is. You ought to be ashamed of yourself.'

'I never—' Amy began.

'I don't want to argue,' Sophia said. 'Please leave the room.'

Amy obeyed. She was surprised at Sophia's sharpness, and quite afraid of her.

Sophia herself was quite shocked at Amy's outrageous behaviour. 'If she does this while I am here, what does she do when I am not?' she wondered. 'Do you allow her to talk to you like that?' she asked Constance.

'Oh, Amy has been with me such a long time. Of course I really ought not to allow it,' Constance remarked unhappily.

Sophia was rather relieved to hear Constance also thought Amy's behaviour was not good. 'Well, I do hope you won't think I was making trouble,' she said, 'but it was too much for me—' She stopped.

'You were quite right,' said Constance, and she smiled a little. There was so much about Sophia, now fifty-one, that reminded her of the passionate girl of fifteen.

'I am sure that servants don't understand kindness and patience. You have to be firm with them,' said Sophia. 'If you aren't, this sort of thing just grows and grows until they do exactly as they please.'

'You're quite right,' Constance said. But it was Amy's suggestions of extra work that had angered her most. Amy had shamed Constance as a hostess.

Sophia then told Constance about Amy and the dogs.

'I should never have dreamt of mentioning such things,' she said when she had finished, 'but in the present conditions I felt it would be right for you to know.' Constance nodded her head in agreement.

Later that day, when Sophia came down from her room, Constance whispered, 'She's given notice! And on a Sunday too! I have a month to find a new servant!'

# 11
# The Riddle of Life

### Sophia's new idea

A week before Easter, the guests at the Rutland Hotel in Buxton were having tea when two middle-aged ladies and two dogs arrived. The two ladies made rather a good impression because of the dogs. It is not everyone who has the courage to bring dogs into an expensive private hotel. The shorter and fatter of the two ladies did not seem particularly important to the other hotel guests, but the taller lady was handsome, well dressed, and quickly showed by her manner and her commanding voice that she was used to giving orders that were obeyed.

She curtly asked one of the pageboys for the manager. The manager's wife came quickly down the stairs, and was clearly respectful. It was obvious that the ladies were wealthy.

Not many of the guests in the Rutland Hotel had a bedroom each, and also a beautifully furnished private sitting room. There were only four of those, compared with fifty bedrooms.

Sophia had won again. She had decided to do something, and she had done it. Constance had agreed to Sophia's suggestion that after they had found a new servant, they should go to stay in a hotel for a while.

They had advertised for a servant in the newspaper, but that had been a failure. A few answers had been received but not at all of a satisfactory kind.

Constance, much more than Sophia, had been amazed by the behaviour and the demands of modern servants. She was in despair. If she had not been so proud, she would have suggested to Sophia that Amy should be asked to stay on. But the thought of having to apologize to Amy for accepting her notice was too much for Constance; she would rather have accepted a rude modern girl than do that.

Then Maria Critchlow told Constance about a servant who could be trusted, and who was soon going to leave a place where she had worked for eight years. Constance did not think that a servant who was recommended by Maria Critchlow would suit her, but when they saw the girl, whose name was Rose, both she and Sophia were pleased with her. The only problem had been that Rose would not be free until about a month after Amy had left. Rose wanted to take a few weeks' holiday with her married sister in Manchester before starting her new job.

What could the sisters do with no one to help them in the house for a month? Sophia thought it would be a big mistake to risk losing Rose by refusing to allow her her holiday, and anyway they had found no one who could start at once. That was when Sophia made her suggestion.

'We cannot live here without a servant. We must just lock up the place for a few weeks, and go and stay in a hotel,' she said.

At first Constance had regarded the whole idea as quite mad; but in the end she had had to agree. She could think of no other answer to their problem.

## A question of health

On the whole, the sisters were well received at the hotel. At first, Sophia was considered domineering and formidable, but after a day or two, she found that the hotel was really good, and her behaviour changed. The fact was it was so good 5 that it shook Sophia's belief that there was only one truly high-class hotel in the world—the Pension Frensham, and that nobody could teach the person who had made that pension so special anything about managing such a place.

However, Constance was not happy in the hotel. She 10 worried the whole time about her house. She expected disasters. One day, a letter arrived which made her feel that she had been right; it was from the new servant, who calmly wrote to say she had decided not to work for them after all. What were they to do? 15

'I will tell you what I have been thinking,' Sophia said.

'What's that?' asked Constance, expecting some wonderful solution about servants to come from Sophia's active brain.

'There's no reason why we should go back to Bursley. The house won't run away, and it costs nothing except the rent. 20 Why not enjoy ourselves quietly for a bit?' Sophia said.

'You mean stay here?' said Constance, showing her dislike of Buxton by her tone of voice.

'No, not here!' Sophia answered scornfully. 'There are lots of other places we could go to.' 25

'I don't think I should be at all easy in my mind,' said Constance. 'Nothing would be settled, the house—'

'What does it matter about the house?'

'It matters a lot!' said Constance seriously, feeling rather hurt. 'I didn't leave things as if we were going away for a long 30 time. It wouldn't be right.'

'I don't see how anything could go wrong. I really don't!' said Sophia. 'The place can always be cleaned when we get back. I think you ought to go about more. There is no reason why you shouldn't. You are quite free. Why shouldn't we go 35 abroad, for example, you and I? I'm sure you would enjoy it so much. And it would do you good—a lot of good.'

'Abroad?' Constance murmured. She was shocked.

'Why not?' asked Sophia brightly and eagerly. She was determined to take Constance abroad. 'There are lots of places we could go to. And we could live comfortably among 5 nice English people.'

'I don't think going abroad would suit me,' said Constance.

'But why not? You don't know. You've never tried, my dear.' Sophia smiled her encouragement, but Constance did 10 not smile back. She looked worried.

'Oh, I don't think it would,' Constance said in an obstinate voice. 'I'm not like you. We can't all be alike, you know.'

Sophia felt annoyed, but she stopped herself showing it. 'Well, then,' she said, 'in England or Scotland. There are 15 several places I should like to visit.'

'I must get back to St Luke's Square,' said Constance, paying no attention to what Sophia had said. 'There's so much to be done.'

Then Sophia looked at Constance more seriously and 20 with greater determination, but still kindly, as though for Constance's own good.

'You are making a mistake, Constance,' she said.

'A mistake?' said Constance. She was astonished.

'A great mistake,' Sophia insisted.

25 'I don't see how I can be making a mistake,' Constance said, her confidence increasing as she thought about it.

'No,' said Sophia. 'I'm sure you don't see it. But you are. You're letting yourself be a slave to that house of yours. Instead of the house existing for you, you exist for the house.'

30 'Oh, Sophia!' Constance replied awkwardly. 'What ideas you have! I can promise you that I let dozens of little things pass by every day rather than bother myself with them.'

'Then why do you bother now?' asked Sophia.

'I can't leave the place like that,' replied Constance.

35 'There's one thing I can't understand, and it's why you live in St Luke's Square at all,' said Sophia.

'I must live somewhere. And it's quite pleasant.'

'You would be better out of it. Everyone says that.'

'Everyone? Who? Who's been talking about me?'

'Well,' said Sophia, 'the doctor, for example.'

'Dr Stirling? But he's always saying that Bursley has one of the best climates in England.'

'Dr Stirling thinks you ought to go away more—not spend all your time in that dark old house.'

'Oh, does he? Well, I like my dark old house.'

'It's a question of your health. I think it's my duty to talk to you in a serious way, and now I've done. I hope you'll take it as it's meant.'

'Well, all right,' said Constance. 'But I do wish you wouldn't try to domineer over me!'

'Domineer!' Sophia was shocked. She went up to her bedroom, shaking with anger. This was what came of trying to help people!

As she was sitting in her room, thinking things over, the door burst open and Constance came in, blind with tears. 'Sophia!' she wept. 'I know I'm silly, but you can't change me! I'm like that.'

'It's all right,' Sophia answered soothingly. 'I quite understand. Don't trouble yourself about it any more.'

Neither of them ever forgot that scene. Sophia was ashamed both for herself and for Constance. She had been just as silly as she had accused her sister of being. Having learnt that lesson, they returned a few days later to St Luke's Square.

## The new servant

It was nine years later. A new young servant of twenty-three was working for the two sisters. She was laying the table for supper. She was pretty and rude, and had cruel conquering eyes. She was happy to torture her old mistresses, and her greatest advantage was that she enjoyed having arguments. She liked change and her employers did not. She disobeyed orders. She sometimes left everything terribly dirty, but at other times she could be as neat and tidy as anyone. She was shameless with men.

Constance and Sophia never quarrelled now. They would have considered separation a disaster.

The servant finished laying the table, and Sophia said to her, 'Please shut the door after you, Maud.'

5 'Yes, madam,' the girl answered politely, and left the door open when she went out. The torture had begun.

Sophia jumped up and went to the door. 'Maud!' she cried. No answer.

She tried again several times, and then said, 'Either she
10 shuts this door, or she leaves the house at once, even if I have to fetch a policeman.'

She went down to the kitchen and said, 'Maud, did you hear me call you?'

'No, madam,' Maud replied bluntly.

15 'You liar!' thought Sophia. Then she looked Maud directly in the eyes and said, sternly, 'I asked you to shut the sitting room door. Please do so.'

If Maud could have bought the moral strength to disobey Sophia, she would have given a week's wages for it. There
20 was no good reason why she should obey. She could easily have knocked Sophia to the ground. But there was something about the way Sophia looked at her that forced her, however unwillingly, to do as she had been told. Sophia had risked everything and this time she had won.

25 Although the crisis was over, neither Sophia nor Constance could eat when Maud brought in the food. But Sophia was not quite finished. As she looked at the plate of food she could not eat, she decided that she would not allow Maud the pleasure of thinking that her bad behaviour had
30 spoilt their appetites. Sophia took some of the food off the plate, and hid it.

## A telegram

The next afternoon, the sisters looked out of the sitting room window and saw Dr Stirling's car speeding down the square.

35 'I do hope he'll come and see us,' said Constance, and sighed.

Dr Stirling had by then been in Bursley for almost twenty years. He was well liked, not so much because he was regarded as a good doctor, which he was, but because he was cheerful, and he listened carefully to everything his patients told him. Constance always felt better when he came to see her.

Dr Stirling did in fact come to their house, and just as Maud was closing the door after letting him in, a telegram arrived. It was addressed to Mrs Scales. Sophia read it, then screwed it up and put it in her pocket.

Later, when the doctor had left, Sophia showed Constance the telegram. It said:

> *Mr Gerald Scales is dangerously ill here. Please come. Boldero, 49 Deansgate, Manchester.*

It was years since Sophia had thought much about Gerald. 'He must be dead,' she had always said to herself. And now she learnt that he was not! Suddenly, her peaceful life was thrown into terrible uncertainty! She had not seen Gerald for thirty-six years. He must be over seventy.

'Are you going to see him?' Constance asked.

'Of course. I must!' Sophia answered.

At that moment, a motor car drove up to their house. It was driven by Dick Povey, who had come to visit them. With him he had a blushing young woman, whom he introduced as Miss Lily Holl. 'We are engaged to be married, aunties,' he announced.

Dick wanted to take Constance and Sophia out for a drive, but Sophia said, 'I'm sorry we can't come. We are in great trouble and I've got to go to Manchester. Do you know the times of the trains, Dick?'

Dick could do better than that. 'I can drive you there faster than any train,' he said. Sophia accepted gratefully.

No 49 Deansgate was the address of Mr Boldero's shop. 'I'm afraid I've got bad news for you,' the owner said when they arrived.

'He's dead?' Sophia asked.

Mr Boldero nodded. 'He's dead. He died quite suddenly. He arrived last night, just as we were closing the shop. We had had heavy rain here all day long, and he was wet through and in a simply dreadful state. Of course, I didn't recognize him. I'd never seen him before, as far as I can remember. He asked me if I was the son of Mr Till Boldero who had had this shop in 1866. I said I was.

'"Well," he said, "you're the only relative I've got. My name's Gerald Scales. My mother was your father's cousin. Can you do anything for me?" I could see he was very ill. I brought him in, and when I realized that he couldn't eat or drink, I thought I'd better send for the doctor. The doctor said he had pneumonia, and ordered him to bed. He died at one o'clock this afternoon.'

Mr Boldero took Sophia into the room where Gerald lay. She was trembling. She looked at her husband. His face was the face of an old man, and this surprised her. She had never imagined Gerald as old, but always as young and proud and strong. Now he was wrinkled and thin, and he looked completely exhausted. 'How tired he must have been,' she kept thinking.

Sophia then experienced a pure emotion that had nothing to do with any sense of morality or religion she may have had. She was not sorry that Gerald had wasted his life, nor that he had behaved shamefully to her. What he had been, and what he had done, was all in the past. The only thing of any importance to her now was that he had once been young, and that he had grown old, and that he was now dead. That was all. The whole of her huge and bitter complaint against him fell to pieces.

She looked up. In the mirror she saw, standing by the bed, a tall sad woman who had once been young, and was now old. He and she had loved, and burnt, and quarrelled in the glittering pride of youth. But time had worn them out.

'What is the meaning of it all?' she asked herself. It was this riddle of life that was puzzling and killing her. 'My life has been too terrible. I wish I was dead too. I have been through too much and I cannot stand it. I do not want to die, but I wish I was dead.'

## What use had it been?

There was a gentle knock at the door, and Mr Boldero came in. 'I should like you to come downstairs now,' he said quietly.

On a chair in the room downstairs, Sophia saw a small pile of clothes. They were badly creased and still damp. The collar of the shirt was black with dirt. The boots were like those that the poorest beggars wear.

'No luggage or anything, of course,' Sophia mumbled.

'No. Nothing.'

Soon afterwards, Dick and Lily came back with the car and Sophia had to leave.

On the way home, the car had a flat tyre, and they had to stop. When Lily looked at Sophia, she saw that she was unconscious. She felt Sophia's heart. It was still beating. They tried to bring her back to consciousness, but could not.

'We'll go straight home as quickly as we can on three tyres,' said Dick. There was no time to lose.

When they reached the house and Constance saw Sophia, she bore the shock well, and helped to carry her in and put her on a sofa. Then Dick went to fetch the doctor.

The extraordinary suddenness of the thing was what chiefly struck Constance, though it did not crush her completely. Less than six hours before, she and Sophia had been living a peaceful, even a boring life. Now the threatening Gerald Scales had reappeared, and Sophia lay on the sofa, strangely and terrifyingly still. Sophia was conscious now, but she could not speak or move her body. She looked strained as if she were deeply grieving.

Dr Stirling arrived. After examining Sophia, he sent Dick to get a certain kind of medicine from Mr Critchlow. This did not help, so the doctor decided to try electricity. Dick drove him back to his surgery to get the apparatus. When he returned with it, the doctor tried again and again, but it did not help. Sophia's mouth and throat were paralysed. At half past twelve, the doctor rose slowly. He looked sad and tired.

'It's over?' Constance asked.

The doctor nodded.

When Maud, who had been so difficult with Sophia, heard the news, she began to sob loudly, crying out, through her tears, that Sophia had been the most excellent mistress a servant had ever had. It was decided that Lily should spend the night with Constance.

Constance could not sleep that night. For hours she lay awake, thinking of Sophia and her life. What use had all that charm and beauty, all that arrogance and audacity been? Sophia had enjoyed a brief moment of passion, and then spent nearly thirty years of her life managing a boarding house. What had she achieved? She had been a businesswoman, but she had never had a child. She had never known the joy or the pain of being a mother. She had never had a real home until she had returned to Bursley. And this is how it had all ended. To Constance, Sophia's life was a tragedy. Constance pitied her.

# 12
# The End of Constance

### The gifts

One June afternoon about twelve months later, Lily Holl walked into Mrs Povey's sitting room, and found there a calm, rather cheerful elderly lady who was now very fat. Her chief enemies were her sciatica and rheumatism. 5

Everybody thought that Constance had come through the terrible affair of Sophia's death very well indeed. She was now more cheerful and sweeter than she had been for many years. The truth was that, although losing Sophia had given her real and permanent sorrow, it had also been a relief to 10 her. When Constance was over fifty, the energetic and masterful Sophia had burst in on her peaceful life and greatly disturbed her old habits. Certainly Constance had fought Sophia on the main point, that of staying in St Luke's Square, and had won; but on a hundred other less important points 15 she had either lost or not fought at all. The death of Mrs Scales had put an end to all strain, and Constance became once more mistress in her own house.

When Lily came in, Constance was putting a photograph into a photograph album.

'Mary has just given it to me,' whispered Constance. Mary was the latest and best of Constance's servants, a really excellent creature of thirty. They got on well together.

It was a photograph of Sophia, and showed her sitting on top of a small windy hill.

'It's just like Mrs Scales—I can see that,' said Lily.

'Yes,' said Constance, 'whenever there was a wind, she always stood like that, and took long deep breaths.' Talking of Sophia's habits always brought back to Constance's mind the memory of the whole woman.

'It's not at all like ordinary photographs,' said Lily enthusiastically. 'There's something special about that one. I don't think I ever saw a photograph like it.'

'I've got another copy of it in my bedroom,' said Constance. 'I'll give you this one.'

'Oh, Mrs Povey, I couldn't think—' said Lily.

'Yes, yes!' cried Constance.

'Oh, thank you!' said Lily.

'And that reminds me ...' said Constance, getting up with great difficulty and going out of the room. She came back in a minute with the box in which she kept her jewels.

'I've always intended to give you this,' she said, taking a beautiful brooch out of the box. 'I don't seem to want to wear it myself, and I should like to see you wearing it. It was my mother's.'

Lily said she was delighted with the gift, and they kissed. Then with trembling hands Constance pinned the brooch at Lily's neck.

She thought of Lily as an almost perfect girl, who had become the favourite of her old age.

'What a beautiful old watch!' said Lily as they searched the rest of the box together. 'And the chain that belongs to it!'

'That was Father's,' said Constance. 'When it didn't agree  5
with the clock on the Town Hall, he used to say, "It's the Town Hall that is wrong." And he was always right. I've been thinking of giving that watch and chain to Dick.'

'Have you?' said Lily.

'Yes. It's just as good as when Father wore it. My husband  10
Mr Povey would never wear it. He preferred his own. And Cyril is like him in that. I've almost decided to give the watch and chain to Dick—if he behaves himself. Does he still want to go up in balloons?' said Constance.

Lily gave a guilty smile. 'Oh, yes!'  15

'Well,' said Constance, 'that's terrible! I wonder that you let him do it, my dear.'

'But how can I stop him? I have no control over him.'

'But do you mean to say that he'd still do it if you told him seriously you didn't want him to?'  20

'Yes. So I shan't tell him.'

'And what's Dick doing this afternoon?' asked Constance.

'He's gone to Birmingham to sell two trucks. He won't be back till tomorrow,' replied Lily.

But Lily was wrong. At exactly that moment, she heard  25
the sound of a car in the square. She jumped up and looked out of the window. It was Dick's car.

'Why!' she cried. 'He's here now!'

Dick hurried in, and said happily, 'I've sold my trucks!' By good luck he had found someone who wanted to buy  30
them soon after he had left Hanbridge, where his shop was. Constance could see that he was pleased with himself. It was his triumph over his bad leg, which reminded him all the time of that terrible event—when, one night, while he lay cursing and unable to move, with a broken knee, his father  35
had killed his mother. Who would dream, when looking at his laughing young face, that he had once passed through such a thing?

Dick rubbed his hands together happily.

'And I got a good price for them!' he went on.

'I must go and see about tea,' Constance said.

'I can't stay for tea, really,' said Dick.

5      'Of course you can,' said Constance. 'What would have happened if you had been in Birmingham? It's weeks since you stayed for tea.'

'Oh, well, thanks,' Dick said.

'Can I get the tea for you, Mrs Povey?' Lily offered eagerly.

10      'No, thank you, my dear. There are one or two little things that I have to do.' And Constance left the room with her box of jewels.

Dick made sure that the door was closed, and then kissed Lily.

15      'Have you been here long?' he asked.

'About half an hour. Mrs Povey said she was thinking of giving you old Mr Baines's gold watch and chain—if you behaved yourself. She was talking about balloons, you know.'

'Thank you for nothing!' said Dick. 'I don't want it.'

20      'Have you seen it?' asked Lily.

'I certainly have! She has mentioned it once or twice previously.'

'If she gave it to you, you'd have to wear it,' said Lily.

'I much prefer my own. I must try to behave myself just
25 badly enough to stop her giving me the watch, but not badly enough to stop her giving us a wedding present,' said Dick.

Lily pointed to her neck.

'What's that?'

30      'She has just given it to me.'

Dick came near to examine the brooch. 'Hm!' he murmured. It was obvious that he did not like it. And Lily agreed by raising her eyebrows.

'And I suppose you'll have to wear that!' said Dick.

35      At that moment Constance returned, and the two young people stopped their conversation.

'Mrs Povey,' said Dick in a grateful voice, 'Lily has just been showing me her brooch.'

He noticed that she was not listening to him, but instead she hurried to the window.

'Something's happening in the square!' she exclaimed. 'When I looked out just now, I saw a man running. I wondered to myself then if something was wrong.'

Dick and Lily joined her at the window.

Several people were hurrying down the square. A man came running from the marketplace with the doctor. They came right up to the front of the shop, where they could not be seen from the sitting room window above.

'It must be on the pavement—or in the shop!' murmured Constance.

'Oh, madam!' said a frightened voice. It was Mary, who had run into the sitting room without them seeing her. 'It's Mrs Critchlow. They say she has tried to kill herself!'

'Maria Critchlow has tried to kill herself!' Constance was shocked at the news.

'Yes, madam, "tried"; but they say she is all right now.'

'I'll go and see if I can help,' said Dick, and he limped away quickly.

## Mrs Critchlow's lover

The whole truth soon came out. Mrs Critchlow was depressed because sales were falling in the shop, which was in no way her fault; all the shops in the square were suffering. The new electric trams that were running now were taking buyers away to other places.

For many months, she had been depressed and irritable. Sometimes she would sit down in the middle of her work and say that she was too tired to do any more. Then she would jump up quickly and force herself to work again. She had complained to one of her assistants that she had had no sleep for four nights.

One day, she had called the eldest assistant to her corner and told her that she had something on her mind that was troubling her. She then confessed that for many years, before she had married Mr Critchlow, she had had a love affair with someone else. Her lover, she said, had been her old employer, Samuel Povey.

There was absolutely no truth in this, and it was never mentioned to Constance. However, two hours after her
5  confession, Maria Critchlow tried to kill herself with a pair of scissors. That was why the doctor had been called to the shop.

She was taken away to the hospital. There it was decided Maria Critchlow was mad. The shop was closed soon
10  afterwards, and it never opened again as a draper's.

All this excitement greatly upset Constance. For a while, she was in a terrible state. She had no appetite. For days she would eat nothing, despite all that Lily did to tempt her. Then one afternoon, Dick Povey made the mistake of
15  mentioning—he never could remember, afterwards, what made him do it—the subject of Federation! Immediately Constance changed from being a picture of quiet despairing sorrow into a positive danger.

Dick was a citizen of Hanbridge, and there a movement
20  had been started which called for all the five towns in the area, including Bursley, to be united into one. This was what Federation was all about, and Constance hated it. She wanted Bursley to remain as it had always been. In particular she hated Hanbridge because Hanbridge, more than any other
25  town, had been taking Bursley's business away.

## Federation

On one muddy day in October, the first battle for and against Federation was fought in Bursley. Constance was suffering severely from sciatica and also from disgust with the modern
30  world.

There had been developments in St Luke's Square that nobody would have imagined possible. Mr Critchlow, who was now extremely old, gave up his chemists' shop and left the square. He let his own shop and house, and also the
35  Baines shop, to a big company which made the two shops into one. The company then covered the new shop with

coloured posters and bright flags to advertise a sale of 10,000 cheap overcoats. Soon the shop was full of customers, buying the coats—not from lady assistants, as in the old Baines shop, but from energetic, rapid young men.

For those who still lived in the square, it seemed that dignity had been replaced by shame. Constance was divided between pain and scornful anger. She even said that she would move.

But when, on 29 September, she received six months' notice from Mr Critchlow to leave her house, because the manager of the new shop wanted it, and his company had only taken the shop on condition that he could have it—the blow was a severe one. Constance had said she would go, but to actually be turned out of the house where she had been born—that was different! She pretended not to care, but the idea of having to find a new place to live in was terrible. In fact, it was enough to make her quite ill.

Meanwhile, the question of Federation was still on everyone's mind. After months of argument, all the towns except Bursley were either in favour of Federation or not interested one way or the other. But in Bursley, opposition was strong, and Federation could not take place without Bursley's agreement.

There were meetings in the market of those who supported Federation, and then there were more meetings of those who were against it. At last came the day of the poll— the day when the voters would show whether they wanted Federation or not. On this day, Constance was hardly able to move because of her sciatica.

## Constance votes against Federation

That evening, as it began to grow dark, a fat old lady with grey hair and an expensive coat could be seen slowly limping towards the Town Hall. Her face looked anxious, but at the same time determined.

It was a miracle, in fact, that she was able to get there. In the morning, she had been almost unable to move because of her sciatica. She had thought it wiser to stay in her bedroom than to go down to the sitting room. Lily had visited her earlier and had been most sympathetic, but she had been rather quiet. The truth was that she was hiding the fact that Dick Povey had gone up in a balloon, and she was worried about him.

Lily left Constance after a short visit, looking unusually thoughtful, and saying that as the day was a special day, she would come back again 'if she could'. She told Constance that she was sure Federation would be severely beaten at the poll. She did not want Constance to worry and do silly things.

Constance continued to be in great pain, as Mary noticed when she came from time to time to see how she was. It was one of Constance's bad days, one of those days on which she felt that life had left her behind.

The sounds of the Bursley Town Band brought her out of her sad dream of suffering. Then she was surprised by the sound of many children's voices. With a face twisted with pain, she went to the window.

She could see in a moment that the Federation poll was going to be a much more exciting thing than she had imagined. Carts were passing by with great posters supporting Federation, and people were cheering and singing as they walked through the square. She could hear people shouting, 'Vote, vote, vote for Federation!' She was angry. Too many people seemed to be supporting Federation.

Constance remained at the window till lunchtime, and after lunch went to it again. It was lucky that she did not look up into the sky when Dick's balloon passed over. She would have guessed at once that Dick was in it, and she would have become angrier than ever. The whole business of Federation was almost too much for her to bear. She could not stand the idea that Bursley, where she had lived all her life, might become even more commercial and modern.

She kept saying to herself that she had a vote, and that if she had not been ill, she would certainly have voted. She reminded herself that it was her duty to vote. She began to imagine that her sciatica was better. She said, 'If only I could go out!' She might catch a taxi, or one of the vehicles that were passing might be glad to take her to the Town Hall. But no, she dared not. She was afraid, really afraid that even the 5 gentle Mary might try to stop her.

And what if Lily returned and caught her going out or coming in! She ought not to go out. And yet, as strange as it seemed, she was sure her sciatica was better!

She decided she would go out. It was less than a four 10 minutes' walk to the Town Hall. She knew she felt much better. She was sure she could go that distance and back before anyone knew anything about it. Yes, she would go. She must go.

Like a thief, she went into her bedroom and dressed. Like 15 a thief, she crept downstairs and, without a word to Mary, went into the street. It was a dangerous adventure. As soon as she was in the street, she felt the pain return, and with it all her weakness and exhaustion. She realized then that her sciatica was not better after all. The streets were wet and 20 muddy, the wind cold, and the sky threatening. She ought to go back. She ought to admit that she had been a fool to dream of going out like this.

She walked on. The Town Hall seemed to be miles away, at the top of a mountain, but she bravely did her best to 25 ignore the pain. She was determined to do her part in the killing of Federation. Every step tortured her dreadfully; it made her grind her old teeth.

This was the miracle that people in the street saw without knowing that it was a miracle. To have impressed them, 30 Constance should have fainted before voting. But she managed somehow to vote, and then reach home again on her own aching feet. A surprised and protesting Mary opened the door to her. By then it was raining, and Constance was frightened, both by her own audaciousness, and of its 35 possible results on her old body. A terrible tiredness made her feel quite helpless. But the deed had been done. She happily gave herself up to Mary's care.

# The death of Constance

Constance had a dreadful night. When Mary came in in the morning, she said, 'I feel so strange, Mary. Perhaps you'd better run up to Miss Holl, and ask her to telephone
5  Dr Stirling.'

This was the beginning of Constance's last illness. Mary told Miss Holl that her mistress had been out the evening before, and Lily told the doctor. Lily then came down to take charge of Constance.

10  'Is the result out?' Constance murmured.

'Oh, yes. There's a majority of over 12,000 against Federation. I told you yesterday morning that Federation was sure to be beaten.'

'You look tired,' Constance said weakly.

15  'Do I?' answered Lily. She was hiding the fact that she had spent half the night looking after Dick, who had been dragged through the tops of a row of trees as the balloon had come down, and damaged his elbow. The other man in the balloon had broken a leg.

20  When the doctor came, he discovered that it was not Constance's sciatica that was worse. She had caught a cold during her visit to the Town Hall, and now she had rheumatic fever, which was much more serious. The doctor did not tell her how dangerous it was. He sent for two nurses
25  to stay with her all the time.

Lily suggested that Constance might like her to write to Cyril, who was on a tour of Italy with some friends. Then she went to the post office and sent telegrams to various addresses that Cyril had given.

30  It was not rheumatic fever that killed Constance a few days later, but heart trouble.

Cyril was not at the funeral. He arrived three days later, and as he had no special interest in Dick and Lily, they were robbed of the wedding present they had hoped to receive
35  from Constance. The will left everything to Cyril.

# Questions and Activities

## 1  The Two Sisters

*Which of these sentences are true? Correct the wrong ones.*

|   |   | T | F |
|---|---|---|---|
| 1 | Sophia was older than Constance. | ☐ | ☐ |
| 2 | Sophia was more beautiful than her sister. | ☐ | ☐ |
| 3 | Sophia was naughtier than Constance. | ☐ | ☐ |
| 4 | At the beginning of the story, Maggie was a married woman. | ☐ | ☐ |
| 5 | Mr Povey was afraid of going to the dentist. | ☐ | ☐ |
| 6 | The laudanum poisoned Mr Povey. | ☐ | ☐ |
| 7 | The laudanum made Mr Povey's tooth better. | ☐ | ☐ |
| 8 | Constance pulled Mr Povey's painful tooth out. | ☐ | ☐ |

## 2  The Traveller

*Choose the best answers.*

1  Sophia did not go to see the elephant because
   a  she wanted to look after her father.
   b  she was too busy.
   c  she thought that elephants were dangerous.    ☐

2  Sophia was able to see Mr Scales alone because
   a  her mother, Constance and Mr Povey had gone out.
   b  he had gone to the Wakes.
   c  the Baines family respected him.    ☐

**3** Mr Baines had died because
  **a** his lips were swollen and black.
  **b** Sophia had not been there to pull him up
  when he had slipped down.
  **c** there was not enough air in his room. ☐

**4** Sophia would not go to the funeral because
  **a** she was meeting Mr Scales.
  **b** her mother and Constance blamed Sophia for
  Mr Baines's death.
  **c** she was too upset. ☐

## *3* The Adventure

*Who did these things? Fill in the gaps with the names from the box.*

| | | |
|---|---|---|
| Mrs Baines | Aunt Harriet | Gerald Scales's aunt |
| Miss Chetwynd | Samuel Povey | Sophia |
| Mr Critchlow | Gerald Scales | |

**1** He became jealous of Mr Scales.

**2** She had gone out when Sophia
  went to the school to visit her.

**3** He climbed onto the wall of
  an old mine shaft.

**4** She asked about the clay on
  Sophia's boots.

**5** She came to spend a few
  days with her younger sister.

**6** She fell asleep dreaming of
   sweet letters from Mr Scales.

**7** He went to Manchester to
   find out about Mr Scales.

**8** She left Mr Scales 12,000 pounds.

## *4* The New Couple

*Answer the questions with the names from the box.*

| | | | |
|---|---|---|---|
| Mr Baines | Cyril | the postmaster | Dick Povey |
| Mrs Baines | Miss Insull | Daniel Povey | Samuel Povey |

**1** Who was happy in his marriage?

**2** Who had thought signboards were
   unnecessary for good shops?

**3** Who was the leading baker in
   Bursley, and a town councillor?

**4** Who learnt to ride a boneshaker?

**5** Who was the centre of Constance's
   world?

**6** Who was preparing to leave this world?

**7** Who took over Constance's work in
   the shop?

**8** Who brought the Poveys a telegram
   himself?

## 5  Cyril

*There are eight mistakes in this description of Samuel's visit to Daniel's house. Underline the wrong words and write the correct ones above them.*

Daniel came to Samuel's house to see Cyril. He attracted

his attention by throwing something through his windows,

and then took him to his house. When they were inside,

Daniel opened a door so suddenly that it frightened

Samuel. Samuel found out that Daniel's daughter was in

bed with a feverish cold, and a broken or twisted arm.

When Samuel went into the sitting room, he saw that

Daniel's wife was drunk. Samuel went to get a doctor for

Dick. Later he left Daniel at the post office and went to get

Constance. He asked her to look after Dick until he could

be taken to the police station.

## 6  The Widow

*Fill in the gaps with the words from the box.*

| | | | |
|---|---|---|---|
| art | citizen | holiday | pottery |
| auction | divide | mess | scholarship |

1  A rich        owned Constance's house.

2  Mr Critchlow bought the Baines shop at the       

**3** He proposed to ▓▓▓▓▓ the house from the shop.

**4** The workers made a terrible ▓▓▓▓▓ in Constance's house.

**5** Cyril worked at Peels, an important manufacturer of ▓▓▓▓▓.

**6** Every evening he went to study ▓▓▓▓▓.

**7** Later he got a ▓▓▓▓▓ to study in London.

**8** Constance and Cyril had a ▓▓▓▓▓ on the Isle of Man.


## 7   The Elopement

*Put these sentences in the right order. The first one has been done for you.*

**1** Gerald asked if she would like to go to the National Gallery. ☐

**2** He told Sophia they could stay in London and get married. ☐

**3** Gerald gave her some money and left her. ☐

**4** She met Gerald when he got on the train at Rugby. ☐

**5** Sophia said she would not go to Paris. ☐

**6** In London they took a room at the Hatfield Hotel. ☐

**7** Later he changed his mind and went back to the hotel. ☐

**8** Sophia asked what the arrangements were for the wedding. ☐

**9** Sophia ran away from her aunt's home at Axe. [1]

**10** He said they would get married in Paris. ☐

## *8* Fever

*Match the beginnings of these sentences with the right endings.*

| | | | |
|---|---|---|---|
| **1** | Rivain • | • **a** | knew of another hotel. |
| **2** | Chirac • | • **b** | felt sick after the execution. |
| **3** | Gerald • | • **c** | stole 200 pounds. |
| **4** | A taxi driver • | • **d** | tried the blade of the guillotine. |
| **5** | The executioner • | • **e** | asked Sophia for sixty francs. |
| **6** | The hotel owner • | • **f** | worked for a newspaper. |
| **7** | Sophia • | • **g** | murdered a rich prostitute. |

## *9* Success

*The underlined sentences are in the wrong paragraphs. Where should they go?*

1 Sophia and Chirac went out for a drive. <u>The concierge said he had been patient, but the time was finished.</u> A woman climbed into the taxi and began to sing. ☐

2 Madame Foucault could not pay the money for the furniture. <u>She said she had to get lunch ready.</u> Sophia said she would buy the furniture herself. ☐

3 Niepce tried to bring a charming young woman into his room. <u>Their wives had been sent away from Paris.</u> She was very angry. ☐

4 Sophia's boarders were all married men except Chirac. <u>Sophia accidentally caught them in the corridor.</u> They regarded Sophia as quite miraculous. ☐

5 Chirac invited Sophia out to lunch. <u>They stopped in a crowded square.</u> But she went out with him. ☐

## *10*  Reunited

*Who said these things, and to whom? Fill in the gaps with the names from the box.*

> Amy  Matthew Peel-Swynnerton
> Constance  Sophia
> Mr Critchlow  The English pension owner
> Fossette

1  'Have any letters come for me tonight?'
　　　　　　　　　　　 to 　　　　　　　　　　

2  'Why not take a holiday for the rest of your life?'
　　　　　　　　　　　 to 　　　　　　　　　　

3  'I went to his house. He's a delightful boy.'
　　　　　　　　　　　 to 　　　　　　　　　　

4  'I won't listen to a word said against him.'
　　　　　　　　　　　 to 　　　　　　　　　　

5  'Oh, get out, you.'
　　　　　　　　　　　 to 　　　　　　　　　　

6  'I don't want to argue.'
　　　　　　　　　　　 to 　　　　　　　　　　

7  'She's given notice!'
　　　　　　　　　　　 to 　　　　　　　　　　

## *11*  The Riddle of Life

*The letters in these words are all mixed up. What should they be?*

When Mr (1) **Bdeloor** took Sophia into the room where Gerald lay, she was (2) **begilmnrt**. She had never

(3) **adegiimn** him as an old man. Now he looked

(4) **deiklnrw** and thin and completely (5) **aeedhstux**. He

had (6) **adestw** his life and behaved (7) **aefhllmsuy** to her,

but this was in the past. The whole of her huge and bitter

(8) **acilmnopt** against him fell to (9) **ceeisp**.

## *12* The End of Constance

*Choose the best answers.*

**1** In fact Sophia's death came as a relief to Constance
because
  **a** Sophia left all her money to Constance.
  **b** Sophia needed to be looked after so much.
  **c** Sophia had disturbed her peaceful life and her
  old habits.

**2** Constance would probably not give the watch and
chain to Dick if
  **a** he did not stop going up in balloons.
  **b** he refused to marry Lily Holl.
  **c** he sold his trucks in Birmingham.

**3** Constance hated Federation because
  **a** she wanted Bursley to remain as it had always
  been.
  **b** Bursley had been taking Hanbridge's business
  away.
  **c** she complained she had had no sleep for
  four nights.

**4** Constance was sure her sciatica was better because
  **a** she fainted when she voted.
  **b** she wanted so much to vote against Federation.
  **c** she was afraid that Mary might stop her.

# Book Report

*Now write a book report to display in the library or your classroom. These questions will help you.*

**Title**

**Type**   What type of story is your book?

- Adventure
- Classic
- Crime
- Detective story
- Fairy tale
- Horror and suspense

- Mystery
- Play
- Romance
- Science fiction and fantasy
- Short story
- Others

**Characters**   Who are the main characters in the book?

**Main characters**   Describe the main characters.
What do they look like?
What are they like?

**Story**   What is the story about?
Remember not to give the ending away!

**My comments**   What did you think of the story?
Did you enjoy it?
Would you recommend this book to your classmates?

Visit the website and download the book report template
**www.oupchina.com.hk/elt/oper**

## STARTER

**The Ant and the Grasshopper and Other Stories by Aesop**
Retold by David Foulds

**The Brave Little Tailor and Other Stories by the Brothers Grimm**
Retold by Katherine Mattock

**The Emperor's New Clothes and Other Stories by Hans Christian Andersen**
Retold by Janice Tibbetts

**Folk Tales from Around the World**
Retold by Rosemary Border

**Giants, Dragons and Other Magical Creatures**
Retold by Philip Popescu

**Heroes and Heroines**
Retold by Philip Popescu

**In the Land of the Gods**
Retold by Magnus Norberg

**Journey to the West**
Retold by Rosemary Border

**The Lion and the Mouse and Other Stories by Aesop**
Retold by David Foulds

**The Little Mermaid and Other Stories by Hans Christian Andersen**
Retold by Janice Tibbetts

**The Monkey King**
Retold by Rosemary Border

**Peter Pan**
Retold by Katherine Mattock

## LEVEL 1

**Alice's Adventures in Wonderland**
Lewis Carroll

**The Call of the Wild and Other Stories**
Jack London

**Emma**
Jane Austen

**The Golden Goose and Other Stories**
Retold by David Foulds

**Jane Eyre**
Charlotte Brontë

**Just So Stories**
Rudyard Kipling

**Little Women**
Louisa M. Alcott

**The Lost Umbrella of Kim Chu**
Eleanor Estes

**The Secret Garden**
Frances Hodgson Burnett

**Tales from the Arabian Nights**
Edited by David Foulds

**Treasure Island**
Robert Louis Stevenson

**The Wizard of Oz**
L. Frank Baum

## LEVEL 2

**The Adventures of Sherlock Holmes**
Sir Arthur Conan Doyle

**A Christmas Carol**
Charles Dickens

**The Dagger with Wings and Other Father Brown Stories**
G. K. Chesterton

**The Flying Heads and Other Strange Stories**
Edited by David Foulds

**The Golden Touch and Other Stories**
Edited by David Foulds

**Gulliver's Travels — A Voyage to Lilliput**
Jonathan Swift

**The Jungle Book**
Rudyard Kipling

**Life Without Katy and Other Stories**
O. Henry

**Lord Jim**
Joseph Conrad

**A Midsummer Night's Dream and Other Stories from Shakespeare's Plays**
Edited by David Foulds

**The Mill on the Floss**
George Eliot

**Nicholas Nickleby**
Charles Dickens

**Oliver Twist**
Charles Dickens

**The Prince and the Pauper**
Mark Twain

**The Stone Junk and Other Stories**
D. H. Howe

**Stories from Greek Tragedies**
Retold by Kieran McGovern

**Stories from Shakespeare's Comedies**
Retold by Katherine Mattock

**Tales of King Arthur**
Retold by David Foulds

**The Talking Tree and Other Stories**
David McRobbie

**Through the Looking Glass**
Lewis Carroll

## LEVEL 3

**The Adventures of Huckleberry Finn**
Mark Twain

**The Adventures of Tom Sawyer**
Mark Twain

**Around the World in Eighty Days**
Jules Verne

**The Canterville Ghost and Other Stories**
Oscar Wilde

**David Copperfield**
Charles Dickens

**Fog and Other Stories**
Bill Lowe

**Further Adventures of Sherlock Holmes**
Sir Arthur Conan Doyle

**Great Expectations**
Charles Dickens

**Gulliver's Travels — Further Voyages**
Jonathan Swift

The Hound of the Baskervilles
Sir Arthur Conan Doyle

The Merchant of Venice and Other Stories from Shakespeare's Plays
Edited by David Foulds

The Missing Scientist
S. F. Stevens

The Pickwick Papers
Charles Dickens

The Red Badge of Courage
Stephen Crane

Robinson Crusoe
Daniel Defoe

Silas Marner
George Eliot

Stories from Shakespeare's Histories
Retold by Katherine Mattock

A Tale of Two Cities
Charles Dickens

Tales of Crime and Detection
Edited by David Foulds

Two Boxes of Gold and Other Stories
Charles Dickens

Othello and Other Stories from Shakespeare's Plays
Edited by David Foulds

The Picture of Dorian Gray
Oscar Wilde

Seven Stories
H. G. Wells

Tales of Mystery and Imagination
Edgar Allan Poe

Tess of the d'Urbervilles
Thomas Hardy

The Thirty-nine Steps
John Buchan

Twenty Thousand Leagues Under the Sea
Jules Verne

The War of the Worlds
H. G. Wells

The Woman in White
Wilkie Collins

You Only Live Twice
Ian Fleming

## LEVEL 4

Dr Jekyll and Mr Hyde and Other Stories
Robert Louis Stevenson

Far from the Madding Crowd
Thomas Hardy

From Russia, With Love
Ian Fleming

The Gifts and Other Stories
O. Henry and Others

The Good Earth
Pearl S. Buck

The Great Gatsby
F. Scott Fitzgerald

Journey to the Centre of the Earth
Jules Verne

King Solomon's Mines
H. Rider Haggard

Mansfield Park
Jane Austen

The Moonstone
Wilkie Collins

A Night of Terror and Other Strange Tales
Guy de Maupassant

## LEVEL 5

The Diamond as Big as the Ritz and Other Stories
F. Scott Fitzgerald

Dracula
Bram Stoker

Dragon Seed
Pearl S. Buck

Frankenstein
Mary Shelley

Kidnapped
Robert Louis Stevenson

Lorna Doone
R. D. Blackmore

The Mayor of Casterbridge
Thomas Hardy

The Old Wives' Tale
Arnold Bennett

Pride and Prejudice
Jane Austen

The Stalled Ox and Other Stories
Saki

Three Men in a Boat
Jerome K. Jerome

Vanity Fair
William Thackeray

Wuthering Heights
Emily Brontë